CANOLA
Gourmet

ALSO BY SHEILAH KAUFMAN

A Taste of Turkish Cuisine

Sephardic Israeli Cuisine

Upper Crusts: Fabulous Ways to Use Bread

Simply Irresistible: Easy, Elegant, Fearless, Fussless Cooking

Soups, Stews, and Chowders

OTHER TITLES IN THE CAPITAL LIFESTYLES SERIES

Arabian Delights: Recipes & Princely Entertaining Ideas from the Arabian Peninsula by Amy Riolo

The Asian Diet: Get Slim and Stay Slim the Asian Way by Diana My Tran

The Family Table: Where Great Food, Friends, and Family Gather Together by Christy Rost

The Kitchen Answer Book: Answers to All of Your Kitchen and Cooking Questions by Hank Rubin

Kitchen Memories: A Legacy of Family Recipes from Around the World by Anne Parsons and Alexandra Greeley

Nosthimia! The Greek-American Family Cookbook by Georgia Sarianides

Sabroso! The Spanish-American Family Cookbook by Noemi Christina Taylor

Savvy Eating for the Whole Family: Whole Foods, Whole Family, Whole Life by Margaret McCullers Kocsis, MD

Save 25% when you order any of these and other fine Capital titles from our website: www.capital-books.com.

CANOLA
Gourmet

Time for an Oil Change!

SHEILAH KAUFMAN
and
SHERI L. COLEMAN, BSN, RN

ISBN 13: 978-1-933102-63-4

Library of Congress Cataloging-in-Publication Data
Kaufman, Sheilah.
Canola gourmet : time for an oil change! / Sheilah Kaufman and Sheri L. Coleman. — 1st ed.
p. cm.
Includes index.
ISBN 978-1-933102-63-4 (alk. paper)
1. Cookery (Canola oil) 2. Canola oil. I. Coleman, Sheri, RN. II. Title.

TX819.C36K38 2008
641.6'3853—dc22

2008011852

Printed in the United States of America on acid-free paper that meets the American National Standards Institute Z39-48 Standard.

First Edition

10 9 8 7 6 5 4 3 2 1

CONTENTS

FOREWORD   vii

ACKNOWLEDGMENTS   xi

INTRODUCTION   xiii

TEST YOUR CANOLA KNOWLEDGE   xvii

CHAPTER 1   *Appetizers*   1

CHAPTER 2   *Soups*   25

CHAPTER 3   *Main Courses—Chicken*   37

CHAPTER 4   *Main Courses—Meat*   59

CHAPTER 5   *Main Courses—Meatless*   79

CHAPTER 6   *Main Courses—Fish*   97

CHAPTER 7   *Salads*   109

CHAPTER 8   *Vegetables and Side Dishes*   129

CHAPTER 9   *Breads, Muffins, and More*   157

CHAPTER 10   *Desserts—Cakes*   177

CHAPTER 11   *Desserts—Cookies*   201

CHAPTER 12   *Desserts—Pies*   213

INDEX   223

ABOUT THE AUTHORS   227

FOREWORD

I've been a fan of canola oil for more than twenty years—long before it became a household name. And, while I knew canola oil came from a plant, I had no idea what the plant looked like. Last summer, while vacationing, I had the privilege of touring a canola farm. I'll never forget the beauty of seeing miles and miles of those chest-high lanky plants with bright yellow flowers.

On the tour I was told that after the flowers fall, pods (filled with small sesame-like seeds) appear. We then participated in our own "crushing." Using a rolling pin, we crushed the seeds and saw the release of all this healthy oil. Just as interesting, we discovered that there is no waste. After the oil is released, the remaining "meal" is used as feed for animals. Have you ever seen those eggs that are higher in omega three fatty acids? Those were from chickens fed this healthy canola meal!

Touring the canola fields took me back to the beginning of my health career—back to when I first recommended canola oil to my patients.

Back in 1980, as a brand-new registered dietitian with a master's degree in nutrition from Virginia Polytechnic Institute, I approached my first hospital job with gusto! I was to counsel patients who had just suffered their first, second, or third heart attack (did you know that heart disease is the #1 killer in the United States?) and I thought, "Now, here are some people who will really appreciate my advice."

Hospital stays were fairly short back then too, so I often wasn't instructed by the doctor to talk with the patient until just before their discharge. Therefore, I often met the patient for the very first time when the patient was fully dressed, their suitcase packed, their family waiting to take them home, and the staff anxiously waiting for all of us to leave so they could prepare the room for the next patient (not an ideal setting for the important work I was asked to do). So, in ten short minutes I tried to do my magic of changing their life! No, wait. I was trying to *save* their life!

Assisted with a three-page single-spaced sheet of Do's and Don'ts (with more Don'ts), I told them they needed to cut back on red meats (and overall meat portion sizes), trim off the fat and remove the poultry skin, switch from butter to margarine, eat healthier oils, eliminate all fried foods, double or even triple their vegetable intake, eat more fruits, add whole grains, reduce their sugar intake, cut out the cream in their coffee, limit the portion sizes of all foods to drop the necessary thirty pounds (or more), eliminate stress in their life, and—let's not forget—exercise every day for thirty to sixty minutes!

I expected a "Thank you" from my patients, but often didn't get it. Even though their loved ones were nodding their heads in agreement about what the patient must do, I often got blank stares from the patients themselves. I remember the day one feisty guy said to me, "Listen dearie, I know you mean well, but there's no way I'm going to change how I eat. I'd rather die than eat the way you're suggesting!" I was floored. This guy had just suffered a heart attack and was given a second chance for life and he didn't want to change how he was living?

It took another ten years for me to realize what I (and most other health professionals) was doing wrong. Even when people really want to change, most of us are not capable of making more than one or two small changes at a time. I learned that important lesson during my doctoral dissertation research on women who had lost weight and kept it off. My goal had been to find out what diet works for long-term success, but what I discovered was that none of these women went on a "diet." While they did indeed make changes, the changes were very small. But, even small changes, over time, can make a big difference! Using this research study as a guide, I wrote the book, "Dr. Jo's No Big Deal Diet" to share their secrets of how they lost weight and kept it off. The title of the book comes from these women. When I asked the women how they lost the weight, they often began with, "Oh, it's no big deal. All I did was . . . "

And, that, is the way to be successful in making any life change. Instead of trying to make every single change imaginable, do just the things that are "no big deal," the simple changes that are easy for you to make.

One of the reasons I'm so excited about the book, *Canola Gourmet*, is because it incorporates my "no big deal" approach to life. Because of its mild flavor, it's easy to use canola in just about any cooking style, including stir frying, sautéing, deep fat frying, and even baking. As a PhD nutritionist, I believe canola oil is the healthiest oil around—and switching the type of oil you keep in your kitchen is such a simple "no big deal" thing to do to improve your health.

Why is canola oil so healthy? First of all, canola has the least amount of saturated fats (the heart-clogging fats) of all the oils. Second, it is also very high in healthy monounsaturated fats (promoted by the Mediterranean Diet). And, lastly, canola oil contains more alpha-linolenic acid than any other oil. Alpha-linolenic acid is a precursor to omega three fatty acid (which is also found in salmon and other healthy fish).

So, make the "no big deal" switch to canola oil. And, follow the flavorful recipes in *Canola Gourmet*.

Joanne "Dr. Jo" Lichten, PhD, RD
Author, Dr. Jo's No Big Deal Diet

ACKNOWLEDGMENTS

We would like to thank all of the family, friends, neighbors, chefs, and cookbook authors who shared their wonderful recipes with us. Thank you for joining us on this groundbreaking culinary journey that leads us forward to better health and tastier lives!

Sheri and Sheilah

INTRODUCTION
THE SKINNY ON FAT

According to the Heart, Lung, and Blood Institute of the National Institutes of Health, over 12.5 million Americans suffer from coronary heart disease (CHD) and more than 500,000 die from it each year. This makes CHD one of the leading causes of death in the United States today. This is in part because Americans regularly consume large amounts of saturated fat, trans fat, and dietary cholesterol, all of which raise the low-density lipoprotein (LDL or "bad") cholesterol that increases your risk of CHD.

Saturated fat is the main dietary culprit that raises LDL in the American population—which consumes four to five times more saturated fat than trans fat in its diet. Still, trans fat and dietary cholesterol also contribute significantly. In fact, trans fat not only raises LDL but also lowers "good" HDL cholesterol, worsening its impact on the body.

Unlike other fats, the majority of trans fat is formed when liquid oils are made into solid fats like shortening and hard margarine. However, a small amount of trans fat is found naturally in some animal-based foods. Essentially, trans fat is made when hydrogen is added to vegetable oil in a process called hydrogenation. Hydrogenation increases the shelf life and flavor stability of foods containing these fats. Trans fat can often be found in the processed foods made with partially hydrogenated vegetable oils that Americans love, such as vegetable shortenings, some margarines, crackers, cake mixes, candies, cookies, snack foods, fried foods, baked goods, and fast food.

As of January 1, 2006, the Nutrition Facts Panel on U.S. food products now includes information regarding trans fats. The FDA has required saturated fat and dietary cholesterol to be listed on the food label since 1993. With trans fat content on the label, consumers will know for the first time how much of all three unhealthy fats are in the foods they choose. The revised label will, of course, be of particular interest to people concerned about high blood cholesterol and heart disease, but it will also help all American consumers make heart healthy choices.

✒ MAKING HEART HEALTHY CHOICES ✒

Not all fats are the same. Fat is a major source of energy for the body and aids in the absorption of vitamins A, D, E, and K as well as carotenoids. Both animal- and plant-derived food products contain fat. When eaten in moderation, certain fats are important for proper growth, development, and maintenance of good health. As a food ingredient, fat provides taste, consistency, and stability and helps people feel full. Parents in particular should be aware that fats are an important source of calories and nutrients for infants and toddlers.Unsaturated fats, both monounsaturated and polyunsaturated, do not raise LDL cholesterol and are beneficial when consumed in moderation. The USDA in its *Dietary Guidelines for Americans, 2005*, recommends that people consume 20 to 35 percent of total calories from fat that is predominantly unsaturated.

What does this mean for you? When comparing foods in the supermarket, be sure to look at the Nutrition Facts Panel and choose items with lower amounts of saturated fat, trans fat, and cholesterol. Don't assume that similar products have the same nutrient profile; similar foods can vary in calories, ingredients, nutrients, and the size and number of servings per package. The same holds true for products of the same brand.

To reduce both saturated and trans fatty acids in your diet, choose canola oil and nonhydrogenated soft margarines made with canola oil instead of solid fats such as partially hydrogenated margarine, shortening, lard, and butter (see Table 1 for a comparison). Also as defined by the FDA, canola oil has zero trans fat and it does not contain cholesterol.

As we have learned that saturated fat is bad for you and now trans fat even worse, canola oil's usage has risen and continues to rise in homes and restaurants across the country. We recommend that you omit trans fat from your diet and limit saturated fat. Read food labels and don't consume foods

Table 1. Trans Fat Content of Solid Fats versus Canola Oil

Source of Fat	*Trans* Fat Content
Shortening	28.5%
Hard Margarines	16.7%
Butter	2.6%
Soft (partially hydrogenated) Margarine	1.8%
Non-hydrogenated Margarine	0%*
Canola Oil	0%*

*As defined by the U.S. Food and Drug Administration and Canadian Food Inspection Agency
Source: USDA Nutrient Database

Comparison of Dietary Fats

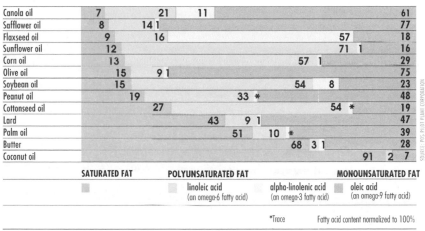

DIETARY FAT

Dietary Fat	Saturated Fat	Linoleic acid (omega-6)	Alpha-linolenic acid (omega-3)	Oleic acid (omega-9)
Canola oil	7	21	11	61
Safflower oil	8	14	1	77
Flaxseed oil	9	16	57	18
Sunflower oil	12	71	1	16
Corn oil	13	57	1	29
Olive oil	15	9	1	75
Soybean oil	15	54	8	23
Peanut oil	19	33	*	48
Cottonseed oil	27	54	*	19
Lard	43	9	1	47
Palm oil	51	10	*	39
Butter	68	3	1	28
Coconut oil	91	2		7

SATURATED FAT   POLYUNSATURATED FAT   MONOUNSATURATED FAT

linoleic acid (an omega-6 fatty acid)   alpha-linolenic acid (an omega-3 fatty acid)   oleic acid (an omega-9 fatty acid)

*Trace   Fatty acid content normalized to 100%

SOURCE: PVS PILOT PLANT CORPORATION

that contain hydrogenated or partially hydrogenated fats. Use fresh and local ingredients whenever possible and get your recommended daily intake— 1 1/2 tablespoons—of canola oil to replace saturated fat in your diet.

This is not a "diet" book. This is a book about fabulous food that is wonderful to eat using heart healthy canola oil. These recipes are tried and true and have delighted our family and friends. Now we hope they delight you!

To your health!

Sheri Coleman, RN, BSN

Sources: Food and Drug Administration, U.S. Department of Agriculture, Canadian Food Inspection Agency, and CanolaInfo

TEST YOUR CANOLA OIL KNOWLEDGE

1. How much saturated fat is in canola oil?
   a. 7%   b. 10%   c. 20%   d. 30%

2. How does this compare to other oils? Canola is:
   a. equal to olive oil in percentage of saturated fat
   b. lower in saturated fat than other oils

3. Do I need fat in my diet?
   a. yes   b. no

4. Canola oil is widely available on the supermarket shelves.
   a. true   b. false

5. Where in the United States is 90% of canola grown?
   a. Hawaii   b. California   c. North Dakota d. Kansas

See answer key on next page.

&o ADDITIONAL FAQS &o

What is a fatty acid?

Fats and oils are made up of basic units called fatty acids. Fatty acids are the basic building blocks of fats, just as amino acids are the building blocks of protein. A fatty acid is a chain of carbons linked together and flanked by hydrogen atoms. Fatty acids differ in the length of their chains of carbon atoms and in the number of hydrogen atoms attached to the carbons. Each type of fat is a mixture of different fatty acids. Most fatty acids travel in threesomes as part of larger molecules called triglycerides.

Types of Fatty Acids

Saturated Fatty Acids

- Saturated fatty acids are found chiefly in animal products including meats, milk fat, and butter. Two other oils—coconut and palm oil—are also highly saturated.
- They are usually solid at room temperature.
- Studies show an association between increased intake of saturated fatty acids and increased LDL (bad) cholesterol. Increased blood cholesterol in turn has been associated with increased risk of coronary heart disease.

Monounsaturated fatty acids

- Monounsaturated fatty acids are found mainly in oils such as canola, olive, and peanut.
- They are liquid at room temperature.
- Monounsaturated fatty acids may lower LDL (bad) cholesterol levels.
- These acids are known as Omega-9s.

Polyunsaturated fatty acids

- Polyunsaturated fatty acids are found mainly in oils such as safflower, sunflower, corn, and canola oils.
- They are liquid at room temperature.
- Studies indicate that polyunsaturated fatty acids have been associated with lowering LDL (bad) cholesterol.
- They include alpha-linolenic acids (Omega-3s) and linoleic acids (Omega-6s).

ஒ ANSWER KEY ஒ

1. **a.** 7%
2. **b.** The saturated fat level of canola oil is the lowest of any commercially available oil on the market today.
3. **a. yes.** Fats play an important role in nutrition. They provide a concentrated source of energy for our bodies, they increase our energy storage and insulation, and they transport fat-soluble vitamins to the small intestine for digestion. They also play an important role in food preparation. They are used as tenderizing agents in baked products, as major components in salad dressing, mayonnaise, and table spreads, and as a medium of heat transfer for frying foods.
4. **a. true.** Canola oil is widely available on supermarket shelves and is being used by more and more restaurants for its health profile.
5. **c. North Dakota.** Over 90% of all canola grown in the United States is grown in North Dakota. Other canola production areas include the Pacific Northwest, Oklahoma, Kansas, Colorado, Minnesota, and Michigan.

- They cannot be produced by the body and therefore must be obtained in our diet.
- They are called essential fatty acids and are necessary for such functions as cell building and hormone production.

Why is canola oils' fatty acid profile so good for me?

Canola is recognized for its nutritional attributes as it contains the lowest level of saturated fatty acids of any vegetable oil. It is high in monounsaturated fatty acids, which have been shown to reduce blood cholesterol levels, and has good numbers of essential polyunsaturated fatty acids. Like all vegetable oils, canola oil is cholesterol free. Nutritional research is confirming that the fatty profile of canola oil appears to be beneficial in preventing and treating coronary heart disease risk factors, including high blood cholesterol and lipid levels, as well as thrombosis.

Why did canola oil receive an FDA health claim?

In October 2006 the Food and Drug Administration (FDA) ruled that canola oil is eligible to bear a qualified health claim because its unsaturated fat contents help reduce the risk of coronary heart disease. The claim reads, "Limited and not conclusive scientific evidence suggests that eating about one and a half tablespoons (19 grams) of canola oil daily may reduce the risk of coronary heart disease due to the unsaturated fat content in canola oil. To achieve this possible benefit, canola oil is to replace a similar amount of saturated fat and not increase the total number of calories you eat in a day."

Can I use canola oil in salad dressings? How about in recipes that call for other oils?

Canola oil has a light and mild flavor and is super for salads because it remains free running when stored in the refrigerator. It also is light in color and taste, and it blends well with many different spices and herbs. It carries the flavors of what you are blending with it and is not overpowering.

When a recipe calls for another vegetable-based oil, such as vegetable, corn, sunflower, or olive,

CANOLA!

OIL CHANGE

Solid Fat	Canola Oil
1 Cup	3/4 Cup
3/4 Cup	2/3 Cup
1/2 Cup	1/3 Cup
1/3 Cup	1/4 Cup
1/4 Cup	3 Tbsp.

you can easily substitute canola oil in its place. Just use an amount of canola oil equal to the amount of the oil called for. If you like the flavor of olive, sesame, or truffle oil, I recommend adding a drizzle of that oil at the end of the preparation of your dish. This way you will get the heart-healthy benefits of canola oil and the flavor attributes you enjoy.

Do restaurants use canola oil?

Yes, many restaurants have announced that they have switched exclusively to canola oil to meet the health demands of their customers, especially in light of the country's increased trans fat awareness. Many restaurants alternatively use a canola-olive oil blend. This usually consists of 75 percent canola oil and 25 percent olive oil. The blends are frequently used in dishes where the olive flavor is desired or for such things as bread dipping. Ask your server if they use canola oil or an olive-canola blend, and if they do not, request that they make the switch.

CHAPTER 1

Appetizers

ARTICHOKE HEARTS
with CHILES, GARLIC, and BALSAMIC VINEGAR

One of the first Smithsonian cooking programs Sheilah attended in 1994 was given by Hugh Carpenter to introduce his *Fusion Food Cookbook*. She became an instant fan and loves all his books and his fabulous food. This is a recipe Mr. Carpenter enjoyed with his wife Teri, an artist, at the famous Napa Valley restaurant Mustards. The recipe, from Mr. Carpenter and Teri Sandison's *Fast Appetizers* (Ten Speed Press, 1999), is simple, elegant, and utterly delicious.

2 (6 1/2-ounce) jars marinated artichoke hearts, drained
2 garlic cloves, finely minced
1 teaspoon finely minced fresh rosemary
1/2 teaspoon crushed red pepper
2 tablespoons balsamic vinegar
2 tablespoons canola oil

Cut the artichoke hearts in half and place them in a bowl. Add the garlic, rosemary, crushed pepper, vinegar, and oil. Stir well, cover, and refrigerate. This recipe can be made up to this point 1 week before serving.

To serve, bring the marinated artichokes to room temperature, place on a serving plate, and serve with toothpicks or skewers.
Yield: 6 to 10 servings

BEAN PURSES

If you love the taste of the Southwest, this recipe from Sheilah Kaufman's *Simply Irresistible: Easy, Elegant, Fearless, Fussless Cooking* is for you. It can also be made in frozen phyllo cups.

1 tablespoon canola oil, divided
1 large garlic clove, cut in thin slices
1 (15-ounce) can black beans, drained and rinsed
1/4 teaspoon ground cumin
5 scallions, coarsely chopped
1/2 to 3/4 cup coarsely chopped fresh cilantro, loosely packed
3/4 cup (3 ounces) grated jalapeño jack cheese
Salt
5 tablespoons canola margarine, melted
12 sheets phyllo, at room temperature
Canola oil spray for greasing

Preheat the oven to 400°F.

In a small saucepan, heat 2 teaspoons of the oil. Stir in the garlic and cook for a minute or two. Remove the pan from the heat.

Mash the beans in a bowl. Add the cumin, cilantro, cheese, and salt to taste. Mix well.

Combine the remaining 1 teaspoon oil and the margarine. Place a sheet of phyllo on a clean work surface and brush with the oil and margarine mixture. Place another sheet of phyllo on top, brush with the oil and margarine, and place another sheet over that. Brush with more oil and margarine.

Cut the phyllo into 12 or 16 squares. Place 1 teaspoon of filling in each square. Bring the corners together over the filling and twist together so that the package looks like a wrapped candy kiss. Pinch the phyllo together above the filling. Repeat until all of the filling is used.

Lightly spray a baking sheet with canola spray and bake purses 8 to 10 minutes. If freezing, freeze before baking.

Yield: 12 to 18 purses

Hint: Canned beans have a 2 to 5 year shelf life because they are low-acid foods.

BLACK OLIVE TAPENADE

This recipe, from the kitchen of Barbara Forrester, the chef at the Parker House Inn in Quechee, Vermont, is a favorite of brewing expert Peter LaFrance, who kindly passed it along to us.

1 cup dry-cured, pitted black olives
1 teaspoon chopped garlic
1/4 cup capers
1/2 teaspoon crushed red pepper
1 tablespoon rum
1/4 to 1/3 cup canola oil

Combine the olives, garlic, capers, pepper, and rum in a food processor. Process until everything is finely chopped but not pureed. Add enough oil to achieve a consistency that is not too runny.
Yield: 6 servings

CHILI PECANS

This recipe gives you a hint of sweetness from the pecans without any sugar and a nice warmth from the chili powder. It is easy to make ahead of time to store for when you need them.

3 cups pecan halves
2 teaspoons canola oil
2 teaspoons chili powder
1 1/2 teaspoons salt

Preheat the oven to 375°F. Toss all of the ingredients together and place on baking sheet, spreading into a single layer. Bake, stirring once, until toasted, about 10 minutes. Let the nuts cool completely. This mixture can be stored in a plastic baggie for up to one week.
Yield: 3 cups

CRAB WONTONS

Because Sheilah's son, Jeffrey, loves Chinese food (especially her crab wontons), he requested a Chinese Bar Mitzvah. Needless to say, she didn't indulge him in his wish entirely, but she did make these wontons months ahead and froze them for the occasion. To reheat place the frozen wontons on a cookie sheet and heat them at 400°F for 5 to 8 minutes, or until hot. This recipe is from Sheilah's *Simply Irresistible: Easy, Elegant, Fearless, Fussless Cooking.*

1 pound cream cheese
16 ounces crab meat
1 teaspoon Worcestershire sauce
Dash of Tabasco
Freshly ground black pepper
Pinch of garlic powder
2 pounds wonton wrappers, room temperature
Canola oil for frying

In a large bowl, mix the cream cheese, crab, Worcestershire, Tabasco, pepper to taste, and garlic powder. Mix well.

To assemble the wontons, place a small amount of filling in the center of each wrapper. Fold the wrapper diagonally into a triangle. Dab a bit of the filling on the outside of the wonton on each side of the mound that the filling inside makes. Lift the corner of the triangle and bend it towards the dab of filling so the wide part of the triangle sticks to the bit of filling alongside the mound. Repeat with the other corner so that the wonton resembles a frog, with the top open.

Heat 3 to 4 inches of oil in a deep-fryer, deep fry pan, or wok. When the oil is hot enough, drop in about 8 of the wontons. If the wontons do not immediately rise to the top of the oil, the oil was not hot enough. Fry for a minute or two until the wontons are golden brown; then drain the wontons well on a paper towel.

Serve with mustard or sauce, or, when wontons are completely cooled, freeze for later enjoyment.

Yield: 100 wontons

EGGPLANT SPREAD

This recipe is good whether eaten hot or cold. It was adapted from a recipe made at the Homestead in Fritz Creek, Alaska. This recipe is from Sheilah Kaufman's *Simply Irresistible: Easy, Elegant, Fearless, Fussless Cooking.*

Canola oil spray for greasing
1 large (1 1/2-pound) eggplant
8 ounces cream cheese
1 cup Parmesan cheese, freshly grated
4 garlic cloves, minced
1/2 cup canola oil

Preheat the oven to 375°F. Lightly grease a baking sheet with spray.

Halve the eggplant lengthwise and arrange, cut sides down, on the prepared baking sheet. Bake the eggplant in the middle of the oven until it becomes very soft, about 40 minutes. Cool the eggplant until it can be handled, and scrape the flesh away from the skin. Discard the skin, and place eggplant in the food processor. Puree the eggplant with the cream cheese, Parmesan, and garlic until smooth. While the motor is running, slowly add the canola oil in a steady stream and blend well.

The dip can be made a day ahead and then covered and refrigerated until use. To serve, scoop the puree on a lettuce leaf and sprinkle with pine nuts, tomatoes, and/or artichoke hearts. Serve with crackers or bread.

Yield: 3 cups

Hint: To eliminate the eggplant's bitter taste, soak the slices in salt water for 15 minutes, drain well, rinse, and drain again before baking.

FRESH TOMATO SALSA

This refreshing salsa, a recipe adapted from one in Sherron Goldstein's *Fresh Fields: A Celebration of Good Food*, can be used with many recipes, like grilled fish or chicken, or can be served as a dip. Sherron runs a cooking school in Birmingham, Alabama, and has authored several cookbooks. Her approach to food, cooking, and entertaining is always fresh. She combines unlikely ingredients and makes them not only work but flourish.

6 large tomatoes, seeded and chopped
2 cups fresh corn, blanched (or 2 cups drained canned corn)
1 cup chopped red onions
1 cup drained canned garbanzo beans, rinsed
1 large cucumber, peeled, seeded, and chopped
4 Anaheim chilies, seeded and chopped
6 scallions, chopped
6 garlic cloves, minced
Juice of 4 limes
1/4 cup canola oil
1 tablespoon hot sauce
Salt
Freshly ground black pepper

Combine all of the ingredients in a large bowl and mix well. Cover and refrigerate until ready to serve.

This recipe can be made several days ahead.

Yield: 12 servings

FRIED GOAT CHEESE
with MINT

Goat cheese and mint are wonderful together. You might want to substitute panko crumbs for the flour for a different taste.

1 (12-ounce) log plain goat cheese, well chilled
1 large egg
1/4 teaspoon dried thyme
Dash of fresh grated nutmeg
Flour for dredging
Canola oil for frying
1 small onion, minced
1 tablespoon balsamic or red wine vinegar
1 tablespoon canola oil
Salt
Freshly ground black pepper
1/2 cup chopped fresh mint leaves

Slice the cheese into 1/2-inch-thick rounds. In a small bowl beat together the egg, thyme, and nutmeg. Dredge the cheese rounds in flour and dip into the egg mixture. Then dip again into the flour. Recipe may be prepared ahead up to this point and refrigerated, covered, until ready for frying.

In a skillet, heat 1/4 inch of oil over high heat until sizzling hot. Carefully add the cheese rounds to the pan and fry a few at a time until they are golden brown on both sides. Remove from oil and drain well on paper towels. Repeat until all rounds are cooked and drained.

In a small bowl, combine the onions, vinegar, oil, salt and pepper to taste, and mint. Toss to mix well. Place a small bed of the mint mixture on each plate and top with the fried cheese rounds.
Yield: 4 to 6 servings

GREEK-STYLE
MARINATED MUSHROOMS

These mushrooms are an old favorite created by Irena Chalmers. They can be served on a bed of lettuce as a light luncheon salad or as an appetizer.

1 pound white button mushrooms
2 tablespoons freshly squeezed lemon juice
1/3 cup canola oil
1 tablespoon white vinegar
1 small yellow onion, finely chopped
1 stalk celery, with leaves, finely chopped
1 garlic clove, minced
1 tablespoon mixed pickling spices, tied in a piece of
     cheesecloth
Salt
Freshly ground black pepper
2 tablespoons finely chopped fresh parsley

Using a damp paper towel, gently wipe the mushrooms to remove any dirt. Trim the stems and place the mushrooms in a small bowl. Toss with lemon juice and set aside.

In a small saucepan, combine the oil, 1/2 cup water, vinegar, onion, celery, garlic, pickling spices, and salt and pepper to taste. Bring to a boil, cover the pan, reduce the heat to simmer, and cook for 5 minutes. Add the mushrooms and the lemon juice and return to a boil. Reduce the heat and simmer 5 more minutes. Remove the mushrooms from the pan with a slotted spoon and return them to the bowl. Boil the liquid remaining in the pan until it is reduced by half. Strain the liquid and pour it over the mushrooms.

Refrigerate the mushrooms for at least 3 hours or overnight so the flavors can blend. Sprinkle parsley over the mushrooms before serving.
Yield: 4 to 6 servings

GREEN OLIVE and WALNUT SPREAD

Sheilah especially likes this on matzoh for Passover. The spread can be made a day ahead. It will keep in the refrigerator for a few days and it freezes beautifully. Make a double batch! This recipe is from Sheilah's *Simply Irresistible: Easy, Elegant, Fearless, Fussless Cooking*.

1 cup chopped, pitted green olives (with or without pimento)
3 tablespoons freshly squeezed lemon juice
1/2 teaspoon crushed red pepper
1/2 cup chopped fresh parsley
1 cup chopped walnuts
1/2 cup chopped scallions
1/3 cup canola oil
Salt
Freshly ground black pepper

Combine the olives, lemon juice, crushed pepper, parsley, walnuts, scallions, and oil in a food processor. Process just until the spread holds together and be careful not to puree. Season the spread with salt and pepper to taste. Cover and refrigerate until serving. Serve with crackers or bread.
Yield: 8 servings

GRILLED PINEAPPLE
and GOAT CHEESE

Sheri was born in Wisconsin, so you will see the heavy influence of cheese in her dishes and appetizers. Goat cheese is so refined, and with the sweet caramelized pineapple, this appetizer just can't be beat. It has a very formal presentation without a lot of work. The pineapple can be made ahead of time.

1 large ripe pineapple, peeled
1/4 cup canola margarine
1/2 cup brown sugar
Finely ground sea salt
Freshly ground black pepper
24 water crackers
1/4 pound chevre (goat cheese)
2 tablespoons honey, warmed slightly

Prepare the grill for cooking. If using a charcoal grill, open the vents on bottom of grill and then light the charcoal. A charcoal fire is medium hot when you can hold your hand 5 inches above rack for 3 to 4 seconds. If using a gas grill, preheat the burners on high, covered, for 10 minutes and then reduce the heat to moderately high. Also, preheat the broiler.

Set the pineapple on a cutting board and cut the flesh away from the core. You should have four pieces. Place the pineapple in a bowl. Melt the margarine and brown sugar in a small skillet over medium heat and cook, without stirring, until it turns nut brown, 3 to 4 minutes. Add the salt and pepper and remove the skillet from the heat. Pour the margarine over the pineapple and toss to coat evenly.

Grill the pineapple, flat sides down, until nicely marked, 3 to 5 minutes. Cut the pieces in half lengthwise and then crosswise into 1/4-inch-thick slices. Reserve 1/4 of the slices for garnish. Arrange the pineapple on crackers on a baking sheet. Top with chevre cheese and place under the broiler until the cheese begins to melt, about 1 to 2 minutes. Drizzle warm honey over the cheese. Serve warm.
Yield: 24 pieces

GRILLED TOMATOES
with GOAT CHEESE

This is one of Sheri's favorite summer dishes. You can use it as an appetizer, side dish, or as a meal all in itself. Sheri has an herb and vegetable garden, so when the tomatoes start to ripen she makes this quite a bit. She recommends using a very "meaty" tomato for this recipe.

1/2 cup canola oil
6 large basil leaves, torn into small pieces
1 tablespoon fresh rosemary
1 tablespoon fresh oregano
2 cloves garlic, sliced thin
4 large tomatoes, cut into 1-inch pieces
Salt
Freshly ground black pepper
1/4 cup dried panko crumbs
8 slices goat cheese, cut into 1/2-inch slices

Adjust the oven rack with 3 inches from the heating element. Preheat the broiler.

Combine the oil, basil, rosemary, oregano, and garlic in a shallow pan. Season the tomato slices with salt and pepper and then coat in the oil mixture. Arrange the slices on a baking sheet.

In a second shallow pan, toss the panko crumbs with additional salt, and pepper. Coat the cheese slices in the oil mixture and then dredge in the panko crumb mixture. Arrange the cheese slices on top of the tomato slices. Broil until the panko crumbs start to turn golden brown, 1 to 2 minutes.

Yield: 8 servings

LEEK and APPLE TARTS

Sheilah's first taste of leeks was via leek and apple tarts served at a Bat Mitzvah many years ago. She must have eaten half a dozen before she asked the caterer for the recipe. The caterer would not share it but instead told Sheilah only a few of the items in it. She went home and tried to duplicate it. This recipe is from her cookbook *Simply Irresis-tible: Easy, Elegant, Fearless, Fussless Cooking.*

3 medium leeks, washed well and drained
2 tablespoons canola margarine
1 teaspoon canola oil
1/2 apple, shredded or grated
1/2 tablespoon sugar (more or less depending on the apple's
    sweetness)
1 tablespoon apple juice or apple cider vinegar
Salt
Freshly ground black pepper
1 sheet frozen puff pastry, at room temperature
1 egg white

Preheat the oven to 400°F.

Cut the green part off of the leeks about 2 inches above the place where the white begins to disappear and discard. Cut the leeks in half lengthwise and then into slices about 1/2-inch wide.

In a skillet, heat the margarine and oil and sauté the leeks and apples over medium heat for 8 to 10 minutes, or until soft but not brown, stirring occasionally. Stir in the sugar and cook, stirring, another 3 minutes. Then add the apple juice and cook another minute. Taste the filling, adjust the sugar if necessary, and season with salt and pepper if desired.

On a lightly floured surface, roll out the sheet of puff pastry and, using a round cookie or biscuit cutter, cut into circles 2 to 3 inches in diameter. Place about a teaspoon of the filling on half of the circles. Fold the other half of the dough over the filling and press the edges of the pastry together to seal. In a small bowl, whisk the egg white with 1 tablespoon of water. Brush the tops of the tarts with the egg wash and bake on an ungreased cookie sheet for 15 to 20 minutes, or until lightly golden brown on top.

Yield: 12 tarts

MUSHROOM MOCK CHOPPED LIVER

As this recipe's creator, Norene Gilletz, likes to say, all that is missing is the fat! This recipe is from Ms. Gilletz's *Healthy Helpings: 800 Fast & Fabulous Recipes for the Kosher (or Not) Cook* (Whitecap Books, 2006).

2 teaspoons canola oil
2 large onions, sliced
2 to 3 tablespoons water or vegetable broth
1 pint mushrooms, sliced
2 hard-boiled eggs
2 tablespoons finely chopped walnuts or almonds
Salt
Freshly ground black pepper

Heat the oil in a skillet over medium heat. Add the onions and sauté until nicely browned, about 5 minutes. If the onions begin to stick, add broth or water by the tablespoon as needed. Add the mushrooms and sauté until well browned. Remove from heat and let cool. Combine the onion and mushroom mixture with the remaining ingredients in a food processor and pulse on and off to process. Serve chilled. Do not freeze.

Yield: 2 cups

Hint: Mushrooms are fresh when the gills do not show and the cap is close to the stem.

MARINATED OLIVES

This delightful recipe is from Sherron Goldstein's *Fresh Fields: Entertaining with Southern Comfort*. It is a great dish for entertaining and is perfect for almost any occasion.

2 cups green olives
2 cups black olives
4 tablespoons chopped fresh parsley
2 tablespoons fresh rosemary
3 tablespoons canola oil
3 tablespoons thinly sliced fresh chives
4 garlic cloves, minced
2 tablespoons red wine vinegar
Salt
Freshly ground black pepper

In a ceramic crock or glass jar, combine the olives, parsley, rosemary, oil, chives, garlic, vinegar, and salt and pepper to taste. Mix well, cover, and refrigerate. This recipe may be prepared several days in advance.
Yield: 4 cups

HONEY CHICKEN WINGS

Both sweet and savory, this is an easy-to-prepare appetizer that the family can munch on in front of a football game or during your next get-together. Sheri's family loves these wings on Super Bowl Sunday.

1 cup honey
1/2 cup soy sauce
1/4 teaspoon garlic powder
2 teaspoons canola oil
2 tablespoons ketchup
3 pounds chicken drumettes/wing pieces

Preheat the oven to 350°F. Combine the honey, soy sauce, garlic powder, oil, and ketchup in a large bowl, stirring to blend well. Add the chicken and toss to coat. Place in an uncovered baking dish and bake for 1 hour.
Yield: 6 to 8 servings

PEAR, GORGONZOLA, and TOASTED WALNUT STRUDEL

A classic blend of ripe pears, pungent Gorgonzola, and crisp walnuts flavors this sophisticated and versatile strudel. This dish is perfect served as an hors d'oeuvre with champagne or as a first course with a salad. Anyway, you slice it, it's a winner. This recipe is from Sheilah's *Simply Irresistible: Easy, Elegant, Fearless, Fussless Cooking.*

1/2 cup coarsely chopped walnuts
2 ripe but firm Bosc pears, peeled, halved, and cored
2 tablespoons brandy or rum
2 tablespoons dark brown sugar
7 sheets phyllo dough, at room temperature
1/2 stick canola margarine or butter, melted
3 tablespoons canola oil
4 ounces gorgonzola or any other similar cheese, crumbled
Freshly ground black pepper

Preheat the oven to 350°F. Place the walnuts in a single layer on an ungreased baking sheet and toast for 5 to 7 minutes, or until fragrant, shaking the pan occasionally to avoid scorching the nuts. Remove nuts from the oven and set aside.

Raise the oven temperature to 400°F.

Cut each pear half into 1/4-inch-thick slices and toss with brandy and brown sugar in a large bowl. Place a sheet of phyllo dough flat on a clean work surface. In a small bowl, combine the melted margarine and canola oil. Brush the phyllo lightly with the mixture, then layer the remaining 6 layers of phyllo dough over the first, brushing each with the butter mixture. Place the pear slices along the long edge of the phyllo, about 2 inches from the bottom edge and 1 inch in from the sides. Cover the pears with the crumbled cheese and toasted nuts. Sprinkle with pepper to taste.

Fold the 2-inch flap of phyllo carefully over the filling and fold the sides over this. Carefully roll the strudel up like a jellyroll, as tightly as possible. Place the seam side down on an ungreased baking sheet and brush the strudel with the margarine mixture. Bake for 20 to 25 minutes or until golden. Remove from the oven. Let the strudel rest for 5 minutes. Slice with a serrated knife.

Yield: 12 to 15 slices

PESTO CHEESE
PARTY MOLD

This recipe was Sheilah's first introduction to pesto. Because it looks elegant and tastes superb, it immediately became an addition to the menu whenever she entertained. Who doesn't love recipes that are easy and feed a lot of people? This one fits the bill perfectly! It also appears in Sheilah's *Simply Irresistible: Easy, Elegant, Fearless, Fussless Cooking.*

1 pound cream cheese, at room temperature
1 pound canola margarine or butter, at room temperature
2 1/2 cups fresh basil leaves
1 cup freshly grated Parmesan cheese
1/4 cup pine nuts plus additional for garnish
1/3 to 1/2 cup canola oil

With an electric mixer, cream the cream cheese and margarine until smooth, and set aside.

Chop the basil in a food processor. Add the cheese and nuts to the processor and pulse until well blended. Add the oil slowly and stop if the mixture becomes too oily. Mix until a paste is formed.

Drape an 18-inch square of cheesecloth into a 6-cup flower pot. Pack 1/6 of the cream cheese mixture into the pot. Top with 1/5 of the pesto. Continue alternating and packing the cheese mixture and pesto until everything is used. Be sure to end with the cream cheese mixture. Cover and refrigerate until serving. Unmold and decorate the top and sides with additional pine nuts if desired.
Yield: 12 to 20 servings

Hint: To keep cheese fresh, cover it with a cloth moistened in vinegar or store grated cheese in a tightly covered jar in the refrigerator.

ROASTED GARLIC SPREAD

This healthy treat is good for unexpected company if you keep garlic and bread or crackers stocked in your pantry.

2 garlic bulbs
A few drops of canola oil
1 loaf French bread, sliced
Warm brie

Preheat the oven to 400°F.

Lay the garlic bulbs on their sides and slice off the top 1/4 to 1/2 inch of each bulb to expose the cloves. Rub a drop or two of oil on the cut surface, smearing it around.

Wrap each bulb in a 4x4-inch square of aluminum foil, bring the 4 corners together at the top of the bulb and twist to close the foil around the bulb. Bake the garlic for 45 to 60 minutes. When you take the garlic out of the oven it will be so soft that you can spread it easily. Serve on slices of French bread and top with warm runny brie.

Yield: 4 to 6 servings

ZESTY BREAD DIPPER

You don't need olive oil to create a tasty bread-dipping oil. The spices and herbs in this recipe make your mouth sing. Store the dried seasonings together in a plastic zipper bag and, when unexpected guests stop by, simply pour the vinegar and oil over them.

1 teaspoon dried rosemary
1 teaspoon dried basil, crumbled
1 teaspoon garlic powder
1/4 teaspoon sea salt
1/4 teaspoon crushed red pepper
2 teaspoons balsamic vinegar
1/4 cup canola oil

Combine all of the ingredients in a jar with a tight-fitting lid and shake well. Pour into a shallow dish and serve with fresh bread.

Yield: 1/4 cup

ROASTED RED
BELL PEPPER HUMMUS

Once you've discovered how delicious hummus is and how simple it is to prepare, you'll think twice about buying this dip ready-made. The red peppers in this recipe, which was created by Catherine Jones, add a welcome twist to traditional hummus. Ms. Jones is a cookbook author and food writer who has a passion for nutrition and healthy, delicious recipes. This recipe is adapted from one in her latest nutrition cookbook, *Eating for Lower Cholesterol: A Balanced Approach to Heart Health with Recipes Everyone Will Love* (Marlowe & Company, 2005).

1 (15-ounce) can chickpeas, rinsed and drained
1/3 cup jarred roasted red bell peppers
1 small garlic clove, minced
1/2 teaspoon ground cumin
1 tablespoon freshly squeezed lemon juice
4 tablespoons canola oil
1 tablespoon tahini
Salt

Combine all of the ingredients in a food processor or blender and process until smooth, stopping to scrape down the sides of the bowl as needed. If the hummus is too thick, thin it with a teaspoon or two of water. Taste, adjust the seasonings, and serve. Refrigerate leftovers. *Yield: about 1 cup*

SANGANAKI

Also known as "flaming cheese," this brandy-flavored cheese dish will delight your guests. Sheilah was introduced to this dish by her Greek cooking teacher.

1 pound Kasseri, Kefalotiri, or soft sheep cheese
1 tablespoon canola margarine
1 tablespoon canola oil
2 tablespoons brandy, optional
1 lemon
Crackers or bread for serving

Preheat the oven to broil.

Cut the cheese into wedges or bite-sized cubes. Heat the margarine and oil in a small pan and brush some on the bottom of a shallow ovenproof baking dish. Place the cheese in the dish, and pour the remaining margarine and oil mixture over it. Broil 6 inches from the heat until the cheese is bubbly and light brown. Remove the cheese from the oven.

If flaming the cheese, heat the brandy in a small pan over low heat, just until it becomes hot. Using a kitchen match, carefully ignite the brandy and pour it over the hot cheese. After the flame dies out, squeeze the lemon juice over the cheese and serve immediately, using two spoons to scoop the cheese onto individual plates. Serve with bread or crackers.

Yield: 4 to 6 servings

Hint: Sheep cheese is available in Greek and Middle Eastern markets.

SPICY THREE-PEPPER
HUMMUS

If you are looking for a healthy, flavorful snack, this hummus fits the bill. Sheri loves this recipe with fresh vegetables, especially carrots, green peppers, and cucumber, for dipping.

2 (16-ounce) cans garbanzo beans, drained
2 tablespoons canola oil
1/8 cup freshly squeezed lemon juice
2 tablespoons tahini
2 garlic cloves, minced
2 slices jarred jalapeño pepper, chopped
1 teaspoon liquid reserved from the jar of jalapeno peppers
1/2 teaspoon freshly ground black pepper
1 1/2 teaspoons cayenne pepper
1/2 teaspoon ground cumin
3/4 teaspoon dried oregano

Using an electric mixer on low speed, combine the beans, oil, lemon juice, tahini, garlic, jalapeño, and reserved liquid in a large bowl until just blended. Season with pepper, cayenne, cumin, and oregano and mix on medium to the desired consistency. Cover and refrigerate overnight to allow the flavors to meld. Serve with your favorite crackers or veggies.

Yield: 3 cups

Hint: Preferably use freshly squeezed lemon juice, but bottled lemon juice can be used in a pinch.

STUFFED MINI
BELL PEPPERS

These are a healthy alternative to poppers. This recipe, created by Amy Riolo, makes a great appetizer or buffet item because it can be prepared a day in advance, baked at the last minute, and if necessary, served at room temperature.

12 yellow and orange mini bell peppers
4 tablespoons canola oil
2 (3-inch) pieces day-old Italian or French bread with crusts,
    broken into 1-inch pieces
2 garlic cloves
1/2 cup fresh parsley or cilantro leaves
1 teaspoon capers
1/4 teaspoon kosher salt
1/8 teaspoon freshly ground black pepper

Preheat the oven to 450°F. Slice the tops off of the mini peppers and remove the seeds.

Combine 2 tablespoons of the canola oil, the bread, the garlic, the parsley, the capers, salt, and pepper in a food processor and pulse to form a thin paste. If the mixture is runny, add more bread. If it is too thick, add more oil.

Carefully stuff each pepper with the filling without puncturing the pepper. Fill each pepper to the top. Coat a small baking or loaf pan with 1 tablespoon of the oil. Lay the peppers in a single layer in the bottom of the pan. Drizzle the peppers with the remaining canola oil. Bake for 10 to 15 minutes on each side until the peppers are soft and slightly browned. Serve warm or at room temperature.

Yield: 4 servings

TEX-MEX LATKES

This recipe was adapted from one on the Divine Kosher Cuisine website (www.divinekosher.com).

1 cup corn
1/2 cup finely chopped onions
2 scallions, chopped
3 tablespoons finely chopped red bell pepper
3 tablespoons finely chopped green bell pepper
1 tablespoons grated fresh ginger
2 garlic cloves, minced
1 teaspoon finely chopped fresh dill
1 teaspoon chopped fresh cilantro
1 teaspoon ground cumin
1 teaspoon salt
Ground black pepper
1/2 cup flour
1/2 teaspoon baking powder
2 large eggs, separated
Canola oil for frying
Sour cream for garnish

In a large bowl, combine the corn, onion, scallion, bell peppers, ginger, garlic, dill, cilantro, cumin, salt, pepper to taste, flour, and baking powder. In a separate bowl, beat the egg whites on high speed with an electric mixer until they become stiff. Fold the stiff whites into the corn mixture. Heat the oil (about 1/4-inch deep) in a large skillet and spoon the batter by tablespoons into the hot oil. Fry until golden brown on each side and drain on paper towels. Serve with sour cream.
Yield: 24 latkes

ZUCCHINI BITES

We love zucchini, and this is just another wonderful way to serve it. This recipe is from Mary O'Hare and Rose Storey's *Recipe for a Book Club: A Monthly Guide for Hosting Your Own Reading Group*.

Canola oil spray for greasing
3 cups sliced zucchini
1 cup Bisquick
1/2 cup chopped onion
1/2 cup grated Parmesan cheese
2 tablespoons chopped fresh parsley
1/2 teaspoon salt
1/2 teaspoon dried oregano
2 teaspoons black pepper
1 garlic clove, minced
1/2 cup canola oil
4 large eggs, slightly beaten

Preheat the oven to 350°F. Grease a 13x9-inch baking pan with spray. Combine the zucchini, Bisquick, onion, cheese, parsley, salt, oregano, pepper, garlic, oil, and eggs in a large bowl. Place in the prepared pan and bake for about 25 minutes, or until golden brown. Cut into small squares.
Yield: 40 bite-size pieces

Hint: A quarter pound of hard cheese, such as cheddar, Swiss, or Parmesan, will yield 1 cup of grated cheese.

CHAPTER 2

Soups

CHILI CON CARNE

2 tablespoons canola oil
1 pound lean ground beef
1 medium onion, diced
3 garlic cloves, chopped
1 (14-ounce) can diced tomatoes
1 (10-ounce) can tomato soup
1 (19-ounce) can kidney beans, drained
1 (19-ounce) can chickpeas, drained
1 cup frozen corn
1 (4-ounce) can chopped green chilies
2 teaspoons chili powder
1 tablespoon oregano
1 teaspoon basil
1 teaspoon freshly ground black pepper
1/2 teaspoon salt
1 teaspoon crushed red pepper

Heat the oil over medium-high heat in a heavy pot. Add the ground beef, stir, and cook until thoroughly brown. Add the onion and garlic. Sauté until the onions are translucent, about 5 minutes. Add the tomatoes, tomato soup, kidney beans, and chickpeas, and mix well. Heat over medium heat until the mixture begins to simmer, stirring often. Stir in the corn, chilies, chili powder, oregano, basil, pepper, salt, and crushed pepper. Reduce the heat to low, and simmer for 30 minutes.
Yield: 8 to 10 servings

CHILI CORN CHOWDER

According to Sue Silver Cohen of Harrisburg, Pennsylvania, "This is the best ever soup. . . . All the Cohen's and Kogan's love it. I like this chowder because its thickness comes from the potatoes and not from heavy cream and it is very easy to make."

1/4 cup canola oil
1 large onion, peeled and sliced
3 garlic cloves, sliced
1 large red pepper, seeded and sliced
3 potatoes, sliced
4 cups chicken or very light vegetable broth (Swanson's) plus
     more as needed
1/2 teaspoon cumin
3 cups frozen yellow corn
1 (8-ounce) can mild green chilies, drained
1 small jalapeño pepper, seeded and sliced, optional
1/4 cup coarsely chopped fresh cilantro, plus additional for
     garnish
Kosher salt
Freshly ground black pepper

Pour the oil in a large soup pot over medium heat and sauté the onions, garlic, red pepper, and potatoes until the onion is wilted (5 to 7 minutes), stirring so all of the vegetables sauté evenly. Add the broth and cumin. Continue to cook 10 minutes and then add the corn, chilies, and jalapeño. Continue cooking and stirring until the potatoes are soft and can be pierced easily with a fork. Add the cilantro, salt, and pepper and cook until heated through, about 5 minutes.

In batches, puree the soup in a blender or food processor, so that it is still a little chunky, not smooth. If the soup is too thick, add additional broth as necessary.

This soup can be made a day ahead of time and stored in the refrigerator so flavors can blend. Reheat it on the stove.

Serve topped with chopped cilantro.

Yield: 6 to 8 servings

Hint: To rid a cutting board of onion, garlic, or fish smell, cut a lime in half and rub the surface of the board with the cut side of the fruit.

FERNE'S HEALTHY BORSCHT

This recipe is a healthy version of borscht from Sheri's friend Leah's grandma. Leah has been a friend of Sheri's for years, and she lives in Saskatchewan.

2 medium onions, chopped
1 cup diced carrots
1 cup diced celery
1 cup shredded cabbage
3 tablespoons canola oil
1 cup potatoes, peeled and diced
2 cups beets, peeled and diced
1 cup tomato juice
2 cups vegetable broth
1 tablespoon freshly squeezed lemon juice
2 bay leaves
1 teaspoon salt
Fresh dill
Fresh parsley
Sour cream for garnish

In a large soup pot, sauté the onion, carrot, celery, and cabbage in canola oil over medium heat until the carrot can be easily pierced with a fork. Add the potatoes and beets and continue to sauté for about 1 minute. Add 6 1/2 cups water, tomato juice, and broth. Season with lemon juice, bay leaves, and salt. Allow to simmer until potatoes are cooked, 15 to 20 minutes.

Add the dill and parsley to taste just before you take the soup off of the heat. Remove from heat and serve. Garnish each bowl with 1 tablespoon sour cream, if desired.

Yield: 12 servings

Hint: A firm, dry onion will keep much longer than one that is soft and moist.

GAZPACHO

Gazpacho is a popular chilled soup of Spanish origin. It is ideal for warm-weather entertaining and a great way to use vegetables growing in your garden.

3 tomatoes, peeled and chopped
1 large cucumber, peeled and chopped
1 large onion, finely chopped
1 green pepper, seeded and chopped
2 1/2 cups tomato juice
9 tablespoons canola oil, divided
2 tablespoons olive oil
7 tablespoons red wine vinegar
Dash of Tabasco
Kosher salt
Freshly ground black pepper
3 garlic cloves, peeled and halved
3 thin slices white bread, with crusts removed, cut into cubes

Several hours before serving, combine 2 of the chopped tomatoes, half of the cucumber, and half of the onion with the green pepper in a large bowl. Add 3/4 cup of the tomato juice. Place half of the mixture in a blender or food processor and blend for 1 minute to puree the vegetables. Repeat with other half of the mixture.

Return the puréed mixture to the bowl, and using a wire whisk, mix the purée with the remaining tomato juice, 7 tablespoons of the canola oil, the olive oil, the vinegar, the Tabasco, and salt and pepper to taste. Cover and refrigerate this mixture until well chilled, at least 3 hours or overnight.

In a small skillet, heat the remaining canola oil over medium-low heat. Sauté the garlic and bread cubes until crisp and golden. Drain the bread cubes well on a paper towel. Set the garlic aside to cool. Crush the cooled garlic and add it to the chilled soup. To serve, ladle the chilled soup into a tureen. Arrange the reserved chopped vegetables and the croutons in small bowls and serve along with the soup to be sprinkled on top of each serving. Chopped hard-boiled eggs can also be used as a garnish.
Yield: 6 servings

JONATHAN KRINN'S
2941 MUSHROOM SOUP

When a friend took Sheilah to lunch at the restaurant 2941 in Falls Church, Virginia, Sheilah discovered this terrific soup. Jonathan Krinn kindly provided her with this recipe.

3 pounds button mushrooms
2 tablespoons canola oil
1 medium Spanish onion, thinly sliced
2 tablespoons kosher salt
Freshly ground black pepper

Rinse the mushrooms well in cold water and drain.

Place a soup pot on medium heat and add the oil. Add the onions and cook, stirring frequently, until they are fully softened but still white, about 20 minutes. Add the mushrooms and the salt and continue to sauté until the mushrooms are fully cooked, about 25 minutes. Add enough water to just cover the mixture. Turn the heat to medium high and bring the soup to a boil. As soon as the soup boils, turn off the heat and let it cool for 20 minutes (this will make it easier to blend).

Transfer the soup in batches to a blender or food processor. If you are using a blender, be sure to remove the rubber center of lid so that steam can escape. Start the blender on low and then slowly increase the speed to medium high. Blend until the soup is silky smooth.

Put the soup in another pot for serving. Season with salt and pepper to taste.

Yield: 4 servings

JALAPEÑO CHICKEN SOUP
with SHIITAKE MATZO BALLS

Jill Sullivan, a well-known cooking teacher who lived in Maryland, invited Sheilah's family to a low-fat, Southwest-style Passover Seder. This is the low-fat variation of the chicken soup she served during the meal. This recipe also appears in *Simply Irresistible: Easy, Elegant, Fearless, Fussless Cooking*.

The soup:
3 pounds chicken, skin removed
2 large Vidalia onions
1 to 3 jalapeños, seeded and finely chopped
3 celery stalks, chopped into 1-inch pieces
3 large carrots, peeled and chopped into 1-inch pieces
1 bunch cilantro, chopped
3 garlic cloves, chopped
Salt
Freshly ground black pepper

The matzo balls:
2 ounces dried Shiitake mushrooms
2 to 3 cups hot water
1/3 cup canola oil
2 large eggs plus 2 egg whites, or l cup egg substitute
2 tablespoons minced fresh chives, plus more for garnish
1 1/2 tablespoons chopped fresh tarragon
1 tablespoon chopped fresh parsley
1 jalapeño, minced
1 1/2 teaspoons salt
1/2 teaspoon cracked black pepper
1 cup unsalted matzo meal

In a large, heavy pot bring the chicken, onion, jalapeño, celery, carrots, cilantro, cloves, salt, pepper, and enough water to cover the chicken to a boil. Cover, reduce the heat to a simmer and cook for 1 1/2 hours. Strain the broth from the soup and refrigerate until the fat congeals on top. Reserve the chicken and vegetables for other uses, or keep warm and return them to the pot before serving. Skim off the fat.

While the broth is chilling, place the mushrooms in a small bowl and pour the hot water over top. Set aside to soak for 30 minutes. Once the mushrooms are soft, chop half and thinly slice the remainder, discarding any tough stems. Reserve the mushroom water.

Combine the oil, 1/4 cup of the mushroom water, the chopped shiitakes, the eggs and egg whites, the chives, the tarragon, the parsley, the jalapeño, salt, and pepper. Stir in matzo meal. Cover and refrigerate for 3 hours.

Add enough water to the chilled broth to total 14 cups (3 1/2 quarts). Bring to a boil over high heat.

With dampened hands, form chilled matzo meal into 8 to 10 1-inch balls. Dunk each ball into hot water to warm it up (this keeps your soup clear), and then add to the boiling broth. Cover and simmer until the matzo balls are tender and cooked through, about 40 minutes. Using a slotted spoon, transfer the balls to a plate.

Add the sliced mushrooms and the remainder of the mushroom water to the stock. Return the stock to a boil and then reduce the heat to simmer. Add the matzo balls and season the soup to taste with salt and pepper. To serve, ladle the soup into bowls and garnish with chives. *Yield: 8 servings*

Hint: Any vegetable grown underground (potatoes, beets, carrots, etc.) should start cooking in cold water. Vegetables that grow above ground (corn, peas, beans) should start cooking in boiling water.

RED BELL PEPPER
and FENNEL SOUP

While prepping for a cooking class at Jungle Jim's in Cincinnati, Ohio, Sheilah saw a pot of this soup being prepared for a party. It smelled and looked so good, she wrangled a taste and then the recipe.

6 large red bell peppers
3 tablespoons canola oil
2 medium leeks, white and tender green parts coarsely chopped
1 small onion, chopped
2 garlic cloves, chopped
8 medium carrots, coarsely chopped
2 medium fennel bulbs, halved, cored, and coarsely chopped,
      leafy tops reserved
1/2 cup dry white wine
2 tablespoons Pernod, optional
4 fresh thyme sprigs
1 teaspoon fennel seeds
4 to 6 cups chicken broth
Salt
Freshly ground black pepper
2 tablespoons chopped basil
2 tablespoons chopped flat-leaf parsley

Preheat the oven to broil. Broil the peppers, turning, until charred. Transfer the roasted peppers to a paper bag or a bowl covered with plastic wrap and let steam for 15 minutes. Peel the peppers, discarding the cores, ribs, and seeds, coarsely chop, and set aside.

Heat the oil in a large saucepan over medium heat. Add the leeks, onion, and garlic and cook until softened. Add the carrots and fennel and cook 5 minutes longer. Add the wine and cook 2 to 3 minutes. Add the peppers, the Pernod (if using), the thyme, the fennel seeds, and 4 cups of the chicken broth. Season lightly with salt and pepper. Bring to a boil, reduce heat, and simmer, covered, until the vegetables are soft, about 40 minutes.

Transfer the soup in batches to a blender and blend until smooth. Taste and adjust the seasonings. Stir in basil and parsley and thin with additional broth or water if soup is too thick.

Serve the soup warm, at room temperature, or chilled, garnished with the leafy fennel tops.

Yield: 8 to 10 servings

MEXICAN CHICKEN SOUP

You can't beat this hearty, quick, and easy-to-prepare soup. The recipe was created by a friend who lives in California, and it is a huge hit in Sheilah's family.

2 to 3 tablespoons canola oil
1 medium onion, minced
2 (14-ounce) cans chicken broth, or 28 ounces homemade
    chicken broth
2 (14.5-ounce) cans diced tomatoes with mild green chilies
2 (15-ounce) cans Great Northern Beans, drained and rinsed well
1 whole barbeque rotisserie chicken, skinned, boned, and pulled
    into pieces
Salt
Freshly ground black pepper
2 to 3 cups grated cheddar cheese

In a 5-quart pot, heat the oil. Sauté the onions in the oil for 3 to 5 minutes, stirring constantly. Add the chicken broth, tomatoes, and beans, and stir to mix well. Add the chicken, mix well, and continue cooking and stirring for 5 minutes. Add salt and pepper to taste. Immediately before serving, stir in the cheese.

Yield: 8 to 10 servings

Hint: If you don't want to cry while chopping onions, light a candle (before slicing or chopping them) and place it near your cutting board. The heat from the flame burns off some of the noxious fumes and carries the rest away from your eyes and workspace. You can also try refrigerating the onions before you chop them (chilling the sulfur oils reduces the volatility of the enzyme responsible for stinging the eyes), using a sharp knife, and slicing the area around the root last (most of the enzymes live in this area of the onion).

ROASTED SQUASH SOUP

This recipe is from Hellmann's recipes on www.hellmanns.com.

Canola oil spray for greasing
1 medium butternut or buttercup squash
1 head garlic
1 tablespoon plus 1 teaspoon canola oil
2 cups chicken broth, divided
2 teaspoons fresh thyme
2 teaspoons curry powder
1 (13-ounce) can coconut milk or nondairy cream substitute
Salt
Freshly ground black pepper
Toasted slivered almonds or pine nuts for garnish
Chopped cilantro for garnish

Preheat the oven to 400°F. Grease an ovenproof casserole dish with the spray. Cut the squash in half lengthwise, scrape out the seeds and strings, and place it cut side down in the prepared dish. Bake the squash in the oven until it is tender, 30 to 40 minutes.

While squash is baking, cut the top off the head of garlic so the cloves are just revealed. Place the garlic head on a small square of aluminum foil and drizzle with 1 teaspoon canola oil. Wrap the foil around the garlic and bake for 20 minutes, or until golden.

When the squash is tender, scrape the flesh out of the skin. Squeeze the garlic cloves out of the roasted garlic head and add to the squash. Add one cup of the broth to the squash and garlic and puree in a blender or food processor until smooth.

Transfer the mixture to a large pot. Add the thyme, the curry powder, the coconut milk, and the remaining broth. Cook over medium heat until warm.

Serve topped with slivered toasted almonds or pine nuts and chopped cilantro.
Yield: 6 servings

SHERI'S HUNGARIAN STEW

World-renowned chef Fritz Sonnenschmidt taught Sheri this modification of a Guljas soup. Sheri would like to thank Fritz for making her recipe seem so impressive in a room full of super chefs.

1/3 cup canola oil
1 large sweet white onion, chopped
1 tablespoon sweet paprika
1 tablespoon smoked paprika
1 teaspoon hot paprika, optional
2 pounds beef, cubed
2 green peppers, cut into small cubes
1 (16-ounce) can diced tomatoes
6 medium potatoes, peeled and diced in 1/2-inch cubes
2 cups chicken broth, or as needed
1 garlic clove
2 teaspoons caraway seeds
2 teaspoons lemon zest
Salt
Freshly ground black pepper

Preheat the oven to 325°F.

In large ovenproof stockpot, heat the oil over medium high heat. Add the onions, paprika, and beef and braise for 20 minutes, until you no longer see any pink on the meat. Add the green pepper, tomatoes, and potatoes.

Cover the pot with a lid and place it in the oven. Bake for 2 1/2 to 3 hours, stirring once or twice. If you notice the soup becoming dry, add the chicken broth to desired thickness.

In a spice mortar, combine the garlic, caraway seeds, and lemon zest. Grind together until the mixture becomes a fine mash.

Remove the soup from oven and season with salt and pepper to taste. Top with the spice mixture, as desired.

Yield: 6 to 8 servings

Hint: Paprika is an oil soluble spice, so you have to add it to oil for its flavors and color to be expressed. If you don't have smoked paprika or hot paprika, standard sweet paprika can be substituted for both. At the Coleman house this dish is served over creamy polenta.

SPLIT PEA SOUP
with HAM HOCK

The Coleman name is of Scandinavian descent, so Sheri's family members have tried to incorporate Swedish traditions into their meals. This recipe calls for green split peas, rather than the traditional yellow peas, but you can substitute yellow if you desire. Yellow split peas tend not to thicken as much as green split peas, and at the end of the cooking you will need to blend the soup to achieve a smooth consistency. Swedish pea soup is traditionally served garnished with stone-ground mustard and with Swedish pancakes topped with either lingonberries or cloudberries.

1 pound green split peas
1/4 cup canola oil
2 cups celery, thinly sliced
2 cups carrots, chopped
1 large onion, chopped
1 clove garlic, finely minced
1/2 teaspoon thyme
2 smoked ham hocks
2 to 3 cups chicken broth, as needed
Salt
Freshly ground pepper
Stone ground mustard for garnish

Rinse and drain the peas and set them aside.

In large stockpot, heat the oil over medium heat. Add the celery, carrots, onion, garlic, and thyme. Sauté for 20 minutes until the vegetables are tender. Add 2 quarts water, the ham hocks, and the peas to the stockpot. Bring to a boil, then reduce the heat and simmer with the cover on for 2 to 3 hours, stirring occasionally.

Remove the ham hocks from the soup and set them aside to cool. When cool, remove the meat from the bones and return it to the soup. If necessary add the chicken broth to thin the soup. Season it with salt and pepper to taste. Ladle the soup into bowls and top each with about 1 teaspoon stone ground mustard.

Yield: 4 to 6 servings

Hint: I prefer to use celery hearts for this recipe. I include the leaf tops, chopped, for extra flavor.

CHAPTER 3

Main Courses—
Chicken

GRILLED CHICKEN
with HONEY MUSTARD

This dish needs to be started ahead of time so that the chicken can marinate. But it is worth the extra prep: it is a real winner for entertaining, and any leftover chicken can be used to prepare a great chicken salad.

1/4 cup canola oil
1/4 cup olive oil
1/2 cup Dijon mustard
1/4 cup whole grain mustard
1/4 cup honey
3 tablespoons white wine vinegar
2 chicken breasts, halved

In a shallow dish combine the oils, mustards, honey, and vinegar. Mix well. Place the chicken in the marinade and turn to coat on all sides. Cover the dish and refrigerate for 6 to 8 hours, turning occasionally to recoat chicken.

Remove the chicken from the refrigerator. Reserve the marinade. Grill the chicken, basting occasionally with the reserved marinade, for about 35 minutes. Serve with salad and wild rice pilaf.

Yield: 4 servings

CASHEW CHICKEN with
BROCCOLI AND RED BELL PEPPERS

Here is a fresh and light approach to ever-popular cashew chicken. Serve over brown basmati rice or rice noodles. This recipe was adapted from one in Catherine Jones's nutrition cookbook, *Eating for Lower Cholesterol: A Balanced Approach to Heart Health with Recipes Everyone Will Love* (Marlowe & Company, 2005).

The sauce:

2 tablespoons lite soy sauce
2 tablespoons hoisin sauce
1 tablespoon seasoned rice vinegar
1 teaspoon cornstarch

The vegetables:

1 tablespoon canola oil
1 teaspoon toasted sesame oil
1 large garlic clove, minced
2 tablespoons minced fresh ginger
3 cups broccoli florets
1 1/2 cups sliced red bell peppers

The chicken:

1 1/4 pounds boneless, skinless chicken breasts or tenders
1 tablespoon canola oil
1/2 cup sliced scallions
1/3 cup chopped cashews
3 tablespoons chopped fresh cilantro for garnish

To make the sauce, combine the soy sauce, 3 tablespoons water, hoisin sauce, vinegar, and cornstarch in a medium bowl; set aside.

Heat 1 tablespoon of the canola oil and the sesame oil in a large nonstick skillet over medium-high heat. Add the garlic and ginger and sauté for 30 seconds. Add the broccoli and red bell peppers and sauté, stirring occasionally, for 5 minutes, or until crisp-tender; 2 minutes into the cooking time, add 3 tablespoons water to the skillet to prevent the vegetables from sticking. Do not overcook the vegetables. Transfer the vegetables to a serving bowl and cover with foil to keep warm. Do not rinse the skillet.

Remove any visible fat from the chicken breasts and cut them into a 1/2-inch dice. Add the remaining tablespoon of canola oil to the skillet and heat over medium-high heat. Add the chicken and sauté, stirring occasionally, for 5 minutes. Add the scallions, the sauce, and nuts and cook, stirring, for 1 minute more, or until the sauce thickens slightly. Transfer the skillet's contents to the bowl containing the vegetables and gently mix. Adjust the seasonings, garnish with the cilantro, and serve immediately.

Yield: 4 servings

ORIENTAL CHICKEN STIR-FRY

This easy Asian dish can be prepared in minutes, especially if you have purchased prepared vegetables or have prepared the vegetables in advance.

1 tablespoon canola oil
1 pound boneless, skinless chicken breast, cut into strips
1 garlic clove, minced
1 teaspoon minced fresh ginger
4 cups assorted Asian vegetables
1/2 cup chicken broth
2 tablespoons soy sauce
1 tablespoon rice vinegar
1 tablespoon cornstarch
1 tablespoon honey

In a large nonstick skillet or wok, heat the oil. Add the chicken and stir-fry until it is cooked. Add the garlic, ginger, and vegetables. Stir to mix well and cook until crisp-tender. Combine the chicken broth, soy sauce, vinegar, cornstarch, and honey, and stir into the chicken mixture. Cook over medium heat until the sauce is thickened.

Yield: 4 servings

CHICKEN and
GREEN BEAN TARRAGON

This dish can be made in advance if you keep the browned chicken, steamed beans, and sauce separate. Just before baking assemble the chicken and beans and reheat the sauce. Pour the sauce over the chicken and bake in a preheated oven. This dish is best with fresh beans, but you can also use frozen. Defrost the beans and cut them to size before sprinkling them over the browned chicken; do not steam them. Serve over rice. This recipe is a delightful combination courtesy of Janet Ballantyne.

1/4 cup canola oil
3 large boneless chicken breasts, split in half
3/4 pound green beans
1/4 cup canola margarine
1 1/2 tablespoons fresh tarragon, or 2 teaspoons dried
1/3 cup flour
2 cups half-n-half (or nondairy) cream
1/2 cup dry white wine
2 tablespoons freshly squeezed lemon juice
Salt
Freshly ground black pepper
2 large egg yolks

Preheat the oven to 350°F. Heat the oil in a large sauté pan, and sauté the chicken breasts on both sides until golden brown. Do not try to cook the chicken all the way through, just brown for color.

Cut the green beans on a diagonal into 1-inch pieces. Steam the beans until crisp-tender, about 3 minutes. Plunge into cold water and drain.

Place the chicken in a baking dish and sprinkle the green beans over and around the chicken pieces. Pour 1/4 cup water in the sauté pan to loosen the chicken juices. Pour out the enriched water and save it.

Melt the margarine in the sauté pan, and sauté the tarragon in it to bring out its flavor. Stir in the flour, making sure you press out all the lumps. Slowly add the cream, wine, and reserved water, a little at a time, stirring constantly to prevent lumps. Season the sauce with lemon juice and salt and pepper to taste. Spoon 1 cup of the sauce into a small bowl and whisk in the egg yolks. Return the sauce to the pan and mix well.

Pour the sauce over the chicken and beans. Bake for 25 minutes. Serve hot.

Yield: 6 servings

BAKED CHICKEN PARMESAN

This recipe is ideal for serving a large group because it can easily be doubled or tripled. It can also be assembled in advance and refrigerated or frozen until it is time to bake.

1 loaf sliced white bread, crusts removed
2 frying chickens, cut into serving-size pieces
1 1/2 cups melted canola margarine
2 to 3 garlic cloves, finely minced
2 1/2 tablespoons Dijon mustard
1 1/2 teaspoons Worcestershire sauce
1 1/4 cups freshly grated Parmesan cheese
Salt
1/3 cup freshly chopped parsley

Using the steel knife blade, pulse bread in a food processor until fluffy crumbs are formed. Measure out 4 1/2 cups of breadcrumbs. Any crumbs not used in this recipe can stored in a plastic baggie and frozen until needed.

Wash and dry and chicken pieces thoroughly.

In a large shallow dish, combine the melted margarine with the garlic, mustard, and Worcestershire sauce. In another shallow dish, mix together the breadcrumbs, cheese, salt to taste, and parsley.

Dip the chicken pieces into the margarine mixture, and then roll them in the crumb mixture, coating well. Place the breaded chicken pieces in a large shallow baking dish, and pour the remaining melted margarine over them. The dish can be made in advance up to this point.

Preheat oven to 350°F. Bake the chicken for 1 1/2 hours. Baste with the pan drippings once or twice as it cooks.

Yield: 6 to 8 servings

CHICKEN BREASTS
CARRIBBEAN

After Columbus discovered the New World and settlers from everywhere followed, the cuisines of these people, their slaves, and indentured servants from China and India fused with the cuisine of the islands' indigenous population to become an entirely new style of cooking. This recipe melds such New World flavors as allspice, chilies, and rum with chicken and olive oil, which the Spanish introduced into the Caribbean, as well as Asian ginger and soy sauce. This was the first recipe Sheilah made from Hugh Carpenter and Terri Sandison's *Fusion Food Cookbook* (Artisan, 1994), and she still loves to serve it for company. The chicken can be grilled on your barbecue or baked in the oven.

1/4 cup chopped fresh cilantro
2 tablespoons finely minced fresh ginger
1/4 cup freshly squeezed lime juice
2 tablespoons olive oil
2 tablespoons canola oil
1/4 cup rum
1/4 cup light brown sugar
1/4 cup thin soy sauce
2 teaspoons Asian chile sauce
1 teaspoon grated fresh nutmeg
1/2 teaspoon ground allspice
1/2 teaspoon ground cinnamon
1/4 teaspoon salt
4 whole boneless chicken breasts, with skin
2 cups chopped mango or papaya for garnish

In a large bowl, combine all of the ingredients except for the chicken and mango, and mix well. This sauce can be made a day ahead and refrigerated in a covered container.

Preheat the oven to 350°F or heat up the grill. Rinse the chicken and pat it dry with paper towels. Place the chicken in a shallow bowl and pour 2/3 of the sauce over it. Marinate, covered, in the refrigerator for 15 to 60 minutes.

Place the chicken in an ovenproof pan and bake for 20 to 30 minutes, turning once and brushing the chicken with some of the sauce it marinated in. Check the chicken for doneness; there should be no pink showing on the meat.

Spoon the reserved sauce over the chicken and top with the chopped mangoes.

Yield: 4 servings

SPICY GRILLED CHICKEN

What could be easier than a dish that is marinated a day ahead, and then just thrown on the grill. This recipe is from the Hellman's website, www.hellmanns.com.

3/4 cup finely chopped onion
1/2 cup freshly squeezed grapefruit juice
2 tablespoons canola oil
2 tablespoons soy sauce
1 tablespoon honey
1 garlic clove, minced
1 1/2 teaspoons salt
1 1/2 teaspoons rubbed sage
1 1/2 teaspoons dried thyme
1 teaspoon ground allspice
1 teaspoon garlic powder
1/2 teaspoon ground cinnamon
1/2 teaspoon ground nutmeg
1/4 teaspoon cayenne pepper
6 boneless skinless chicken breast halves

In a shallow glass dish, combine the onion, grapefruit juice, oil, soy sauce, honey, garlic, salt, sage, thyme, allspice, garlic powder, cinnamon, nutmeg, and cayenne and mix well. Reserve 1/3 cup of the marinade for basting and refrigerate. Add the chicken to the remaining marinade and turn to coat. Cover the dish and refrigerate overnight.

Remove the chicken and marinade from the refrigerator, drain the chicken, and discard the marinade. Grill the chicken, uncovered, over medium coals for 3 minutes on each side. Baste with reserved marinade. Continue grilling for 6 to 8 minutes or until the juices run clear, basting and turning several times.

Yield: 6 servings

CHICKEN BREASTS
ROMANO

One of Sheilah's out-of-town students shared this with her a number of years ago.

The chicken:
6 boneless, skinless chicken breasts
3 large eggs, lightly beaten
1/2 cup freshly grated Romano or Parmesan cheese
1/3 cup freshly minced flat-leaf parsley
Salt
3/4 cup flour
1 1/2 cups plain breadcrumbs
3 tablespoons canola margarine
2 tablespoons canola oil

The sauce:
4 tablespoons canola margarine
1 tablespoon flour
2 teaspoons tomato paste
1/4 cup chicken broth
1 cup whipping cream
1/2 cup freshly grated Romano cheese
1/4 cup freshly minced flat-leaf parsley
6 slices mozzarella cheese

Place each chicken breast between 2 sheets of waxed paper and pound with a rolling pin or meat tenderizer until they are a uniform thickness.

In a shallow pie pan whisk together the eggs, 3 tablespoons water, Romano, parsley, and salt to taste. Place the flour on one plate, and place the breadcrumbs on another. Coat each breast on both sides with flour, shaking off any excess. Then dip the chicken into the egg mixture. Coat the breast on both sides with the breadcrumbs. Repeat with the remaining breasts.

Place chicken in a baking dish or on a cookie sheet and refrigerate for 30 minutes so the coating will set.

In a large skillet heat the margarine and oil until the butter is melted and mixture is hot. Add chicken breasts but let the breasts touch each other. You may have to cook them in more than one batch. Sauté each breast until it is golden brown, 6 to 7 minutes on each side. Drain well on paper towels.

In a 2- to 3-quart saucepan, over medium heat, melt the remaining margarine. Whisk in the flour to make a thin roux. Whisk constantly for 2 to 3 minutes making sure the roux does not burn or turn dark brown. Remove the pan from the heat and whisk in the tomato paste, chicken broth, whipping cream, Romano cheese, and two tablespoons of the parsley. Mix well.

Return the pan to the heat and cook and whisk just until the mixture reaches a boil. Remove the pan from the heat. If preparing the sauce ahead of time, place a buttered sheet of waxed paper directly on top of the sauce to prevent a skin from forming.

When ready to serve, preheat the oven to 400°F.

In an 8x12-inch shallow au gratin or baking dish, place the chicken pieces in a slightly overlapping horizontal row. Stir the sauce to loosen it and spread it over the entire surface of the chicken. Top with the cheese slices and sprinkle with the remaining parsley. Bake for 5 to 10 minutes, until the sauce is bubbly and the cheese melted.

Yield: 6 servings

CHICKEN CACCIATORE

This recipe is courtesy of Sally Bernstein, Editor in Chief, Sallys-Place.com.

1 to 2 cups flour, plus additional as needed
Salt
Ground black pepper
2 pounds chicken, cut into pieces
1 1/2 ounces canola margarine
2 1/2 ounces canola oil
1 large garlic clove
2 medium onions, chopped
2 small green peppers, chopped
1 cup pimento stuffed olives
2 cups canned plum tomatoes
1 tablespoon tomato paste
2 tablespoons chopped parsley
Pinch of dried thyme
Pinch of dried oregano
1 cup dry red wine
2 cups sliced mushrooms

Place the flour and salt and pepper to taste in a large zip-top bag and shake well to mix. Add the chicken pieces and shake to lightly coat each piece.

Heat the butter and oil in a large heavy skillet over medium heat. When the pan is hot, add the garlic and stir. Add the chicken pieces, onion, and green pepper. Continue to stir and sauté until the chicken is golden brown on all sides. Stir in the olives, tomatoes, tomato paste, salt and pepper to taste, parsley, thyme, oregano, and wine. Mix well, reduce heat, cover, and simmer for 1 hour.

Add the mushrooms and continue to simmer, covered, another 30 minutes, until the chicken is cooked through and tender. Serve over spaghetti or angel hair pasta.

Yield: 4 servings

CHICKEN DIJON

This easy flavorful dish is good hot or cold. Sheilah tends to double or triple this recipe because it is good hot or cold and freezes well. This recipe had been adapted from one in Sheilah's *Upper Crusts: Fabulous Ways to Use Bread.*

1 loaf sliced white bread
3 to 4 chicken breasts, halved
Canola oil for basting
Cayenne pepper or paprika
1/2 cup Dijon mustard
6 tablespoons canola margarine, melted

Preheat the oven to 350°F.

Using the steel knife blade, pulse bread in the food processor until fluffy crumbs are formed. Measure out 1 cup of fine breadcrumbs. Any crumbs not used in this recipe can be stored in a plastic baggie and frozen until needed.

Rinse the chicken and pat it dry. Place it skin side up in an ovenproof baking dish. Brush the pieces lightly with canola oil and sprinkle a little cayenne pepper on each. Bake for 30 minutes. If using boneless breasts, cook for only 15 to 20 minutes, or until just done.

Remove chicken from the oven and turn the oven temperature to broil.

Using a pastry brush, brush the tops of the chicken with Dijon mustard a couple times. Sprinkle the breadcrumbs over the mustard. Drizzle each piece with melted margarine. Broil for 3 to 5 minutes or until the coating is golden brown.

Yield: 4 to 6 servings

CHICKEN FIESTA
CASSEROLE

This recipe is the Mexican way to use leftover or stale tortillas.

1/4 cup canola oil
18 (6-inch) corn tortillas, cut into 1/2-inch strips
1 large onion, finely chopped
4 medium tomatoes, peeled, seeded, and chopped
1 to 2 tablespoons chili powder
Salt
Freshly ground black pepper
1 teaspoon sugar
1 1/2 cups whipping cream
4 to 6 cups cooked, shredded chicken (preferably all white meat)
1 1/2 cups grated Monterey Jack cheese

In a large skillet, heat the oil over medium-high heat and fry the tortilla strips, turning once. Do not let them brown. Drain the strips well on paper towels.

Pour off all but 2 tablespoons of the oil, and sauté the onion over medium heat for 3 minutes, stirring constantly. Add the tomatoes, chili powder, salt and pepper to taste, and sugar. Simmer gently until the sauce is well blended.

Grease a large casserole or baking dish. Pour in enough sauce to coat the bottom lightly. Place 1/4 of the tortilla strips over the sauce. Pour 1/4 of the cream over the strips, and top with 1/3 of the chicken and 1/3 of the remaining sauce. Repeat twice, ending with the remaining 1/4 of tortilla strips and cream. Sprinkle the cheese over the top. The dish may be made in advance up to this point and then refrigerated or frozen.

Preheat the oven to 350°F. Bake the casserole uncovered for 30 minutes, or until the cheese has melted and the dish is thoroughly heated. If baking directly from the freezer, increase the baking time to 1 hour.

Yield: 6 servings

CHINESE NOODLES with CHICKEN

This can be made meatless or used as a side dish. Serve it cold or warm.

2 cooked chicken breasts, cut into thin strips
4 ounces firm tofu, cut into cubes, optional
1 bunch scallions, including 2 inches green part, cut into julienne
1/2 cup coarsely chopped walnuts
1 pound thin vermicelli or angel hair pasta, cooked al dente,
      drained, and cooled under cold water
1 1/2 cups canola oil
2 tablespoons sesame oil
2 tablespoons sesame seeds
3 tablespoons ground coriander
3/4 cup soy sauce
1 scant teaspoon hot chili oil, optional

In a large bowl combine the chicken, tofu (if using), scallions, and walnuts. Stir in the cooled pasta and mix well.

In a small pan over medium heat, heat the oils and sesame seeds. Stir and cook just until the seeds turn light brown in color. Remove the pan from the heat and quickly stir in the coriander and soy sauce. The mixture may crackle and sizzle, so stand away from the pot as you stir. Add the chili oil, if using, and mix well.

Pour the dressing over the noodles and toss well to coat evenly using forks or your hands. Serve the dish warm, or place the noodles in a serving bowl, cover, and refrigerate until cold (about 3 hours).
Yield: 6 to 8 servings

FIG AND GINGER CHICKEN
BREASTS with COUSCOUS

Fresh figs, lemons, and ginger are classic North African ingredients. While the traditional recipe for fig and ginger chicken takes hours to prepare, this satisfyingly tangy version can be made in less than 30 minutes. This dish, courtesy of Amy Riolo, is great for entertaining.

The chicken:
Flour for dredging
2 teaspoons ground ginger
Salt
Ground black pepper
3 boneless chicken breasts, split in half
3 teaspoons extra-virgin olive oil
1 (12-ounce) jar fig preserves
1 handful freshly chopped cilantro or parsley, for garnish

The couscous:
6 teaspoons canola oil
3/4 teaspoon salt
2 1/3 cups plain instant couscous
Zest of one lemon

Pour flour onto a large sheet of waxed paper or into a shallow pan. Add 1 teaspoon of the ginger and salt and pepper to taste, and mix to combine. Coat the chicken breasts with the flour mixture.

Heat the olive oil in a large wide skillet over medium high heat. Place the chicken breasts in the skillet. Let cook 5 to 7 minutes (until golden). Then, turn them over and continue to cook until they are lightly golden on each side. Reduce the heat to low to keep the chicken warm.

Mix the remaining ginger into the fig preserves and add to the skillet, on top of the chicken. Cover the skillet and cook for 10 to 15 minutes, until the preserves form a sauce.

Meanwhile, make the couscous. Bring 3 cups water, 1 teaspoon of the oil, and the salt to a boil in a saucepan. Remove the saucepan from the heat, add the couscous, stir, and cover with a tight-fitting lid. Allow the couscous to stand for 7 minutes. Fluff with a fork, and then add the remaining oil and the lemon zest. Stir to incorporate.

Divide equal portions of the couscous onto 6 plates. Top with the chicken and garnish with cilantro or parsley. Serve immediately.
Yield: 6 servings

MANGO CHICKEN QUESADILLAS

This recipe can be used as an appetizer or main course. Just make sure you have enough! You can substitute papaya for mango or use a combination of both of them. The chicken can be left out, if you prefer.

1 (7-ounce) jar roasted red pepper, drained
1 teaspoon chipotle chilies in adobo sauce or a dash of hot sauce
4 (9- or 10-inch) flour tortillas
4 tablespoons pesto, plus additional as needed
1 large mango, peeled and chopped
2 cups grated Monterey Jack or pepper Jack cheese
2 cups poached sliced chicken breasts
2 tablespoons canola margarine, divided
1 or 2 tablespoons canola oil, divided

Preheat the oven to 375°F.

In a food processor, blend the peppers and the chilies until smooth. Place the mixture in a small bowl. This can be done ahead, covered, and refrigerated until needed.

Place the tortillas on a work surface and brush 1 tablespoon of pesto over half of each tortilla. Place a few slices of chicken on the pesto. Sprinkle 1/4 of the cheese and mangos over the chicken on each tortilla. Fold the empty half of each tortilla over the cheese and mango.

In a large skillet over medium heat, melt 1 tablespoon of the margarine with 1 tablespoon of the oil. Cook the quesadillas until golden brown on each side, adding more margarine and oil as needed.

Transfer quesadillas to a large baking sheet and brush the tops with the red pepper mixture. Bake the quesadillas until the cheese melts and tortillas are crisp, 5 to 10 minutes.

Cut each quesadilla into 6 wedges and serve with salsa and sour cream.
Yield: 2 to 4 servings

LAYERED SOUTHWEST CHICKEN SALAD

This dish is perfect for a buffet.

The salad:
1 head Romaine lettuce, washed, dried, and torn into pieces
2 pounds boneless, skinless chicken, poached, chilled and
    chopped
3 to 4 large tomatoes, chopped
1 (13-ounce) can black olives, drained and sliced
1/2 cup chopped scallions
2 cups grated extra-sharp cheddar cheese
1 can hearts of palm, drained and sliced in 1/2-inch slices
1 (14-ounce) can artichoke hearts packed in water, drained and
    cut into quarters
10 slices bacon, cooked, drained, and crumbled, optional
2 cups crushed tortilla chips

The dressing:
2 teaspoons minced garlic cloves
3 ripe avocados, peeled
5 tablespoons freshly squeezed lemon juice
1 1/2 cups sour cream
1/2 cup canola oil
1/ 2 to 1 teaspoon chili powder
Salt, optional
Freshly ground black pepper
1/2 teaspoon ground cumin
1/4 teaspoon hot sauce, plus additional to taste, optional

In a large deep bowl, layer the lettuce, chicken, tomatoes, olives, scallions, cheese, hearts of palm, artichoke hearts, and bacon if using. Cover the bowl and refrigerate until ready to serve. The dish can be made up to this point up to 12 hours in advance.

To prepare the dressing, place the steel knife in the food processor and add the garlic, avocados, lemon juice, and sour cream. Process until the mixture is smooth. Add the oil, chili powder, salt if using, pepper, cumin, and hot sauce. Process until well blended. (The dressing will be runny.) More sour cream and/or oil can be added if needed. Place the dressing in a bowl, press plastic wrap directly on its surface, and refrigerate until needed.

At serving time, taste the dressing, adjust the seasoning if needed, and pour over the salad. Top with the crushed tortilla chips. Serve immediately.

Yield: 10 to 12 servings

SPICE-IT-UP
ORANGE CHICKEN

This is a flavorful family favorite and can easily be made with beef instead of chicken. Just substitute 1 pound of thinly sliced flank or round steak and beef broth for the chicken breast and broth.

2 tablespoons canola oil
1 pound chicken breast, skinned, boned, and cubed
1/4 cup orange zest
1 garlic clove, minced
1/2 teaspoon grated fresh ginger
2 tablespoons cornstarch
1 cup chicken broth
1/4 cup soy sauce
1/4 cup dry sherry
1/4 cup orange marmalade
1/4 to 1/2 teaspoon crushed red pepper

In a large skillet over medium-high heat, heat the oil. Add the chicken and fry for 3 minutes, until golden brown on all sides. Add the orange zest, garlic, and ginger. Stir-fry for 1 minute. Add all of the remaining ingredients, bring everything to a boil over medium heat, and stir for 1 minute. Serve over brown rice.

Yield: 2 to 3 servings

MACARONI WITH CHICKEN
(Lisan al Asfur bil Firakh)

This is an Egyptian baked chicken and pasta dish popular throughout the Mediterranean region. Egyptian Jews prepare this dish as part of the Friday Sabbath meal. Some Egyptian Muslims eat it on the first day of Muharram, the first month of the Islamic calendar. The chicken and sauce can be made a day in advance to cut down on preparation time. This recipe is courtesy of Amy Riolo.

The chicken:
1 (3 to 3 1/2 pound) whole chicken
1 tablespoon canola oil
Salt
Freshly ground black pepper
1 onion, quartered
4 garlic cloves, peeled
1 teaspoon cardamom
1 teaspoon ground ginger
1 teaspoon coriander

The tomato sauce:
1 tablespoon olive oil
2 garlic cloves, finely chopped
3 cups canned tomato puree
2 teaspoons chopped fresh parsley
1/2 teaspoon salt
1/4 teaspoon pepper

The pasta:
1 pound orzo pasta
1 tablespoon canola oil
1/8 cup green olives, pitted and roughly chopped
1 teaspoon chopped fresh cilantro, for garnish

Preheat the oven to 425°F. Rinse the chicken and pat it dry. Use 1 tablespoon of the oil to coat the chicken and place the bird in an ovenproof baking pan. Season with salt and pepper to taste. Stuff the onion and 4 of the garlic cloves into the chicken cavity.

In a small bowl, combine the cardamom, ginger, and coriander. Rub the spice mix on the chicken. Bake the bird for 1 1/2 hours or until the thigh juices run clear when the chicken is pierced with a fork. (This may be done a day in advance.)

To prepare the sauce, heat the oil over medium heat in a heavy pot. Add the garlic and sauté until it begins to color. Add the tomato puree and mix well. Season with parsley, salt, and pepper. Bring the sauce to a boil. Reduce the heat to medium-low and simmer 30 minutes. Remove the pan from the heat. (This may be done a day in advance.) Lower the oven temperature to 325°F. Prepare the pasta according to the instructions on the package, but drain the noodles 3 minutes early to ensure they will not become soggy in the oven. Toss the pasta with the oil to prevent it from sticking.

To assemble the dish, remove the skin from the chicken when it is cool and then separate meat from the bones. Add the chicken, sauce, and olives to the orzo, and stir to mix well. Pour the pasta into a large shallow baking dish and smooth the top with a spatula. Bake until the sauce is absorbed, about 30 minutes. Top with fresh cilantro.

Yield: 4 to 6 servings

MICHELLE'S FAMOUS CHICKEN POT PIE

Sheri met Michelle over the phone along her canola journey, but the two have never met in person. Michelle has a heart of gold! In this recipe, low-fat or nondairy milk substitute can be used in lieu of the evaporated milk.

The filling:
6 boneless, skinless chicken breast halves
Canola oil spray for greasing
1 large onion, chopped
1 garlic clove, crushed
1 cup sliced fresh mushrooms
2 cups thinly sliced carrots
1 1/2 cups sliced celery
1/8 teaspoon ground sage
1/8 teaspoon ground thyme
Freshly ground black pepper
10 ounces condensed chicken broth
13 1/2 ounces evaporated milk
1/3 cup all-purpose flour

The crust:
2/3 cup whole grain pastry flour
1/2 cup whole wheat flour
1 tablespoon baking powder
1/2 teaspoon salt
1/2 teaspoon sugar
2 1/2 tablespoons canola oil
1/2 cup evaporated milk

Cut the chicken into 1-inch pieces. Lightly grease a nonstick skillet or wok with spray and heat on medium-high until hot. Add 1/2 of the chicken pieces, searing just until the chicken starts to brown. Remove the chicken with a slotted spoon into a lightly greased 3-quart casserole dish. Repeat with the remaining chicken.

In the same skillet, sauté the onion, garlic, and mushrooms until the onion is soft, 3 to 5 minutes. Add the carrot, celery, sage, thyme, and pepper and stir-fry for 2 minutes. Then add the chicken broth. Bring the mixture to a boil. Reduce the heat. Simmer, covered, for 20 minutes, until the carrots are tender. Combine the evaporated milk and flour in a shaker and shake until they are smooth. Pour slowly into the skillet and stir until the mixture boils and thickens. Pour the sauce and vegetables over the chicken. Stir to combine.

Preheat the oven to 425°F.

To prepare the crust, combine the flours, baking powder, salt, and sugar in a medium bowl. Stir in the oil until well mixed. Stir in the evaporated milk with a fork until all the flour is moist. Knead the dough 8 to 10 times on a lightly floured surface. Then pat or roll out the dough into the shape of the top of the casserole dish. Cut the dough into wedges or squares and lay the pieces on top of the casserole. Bake, uncovered, for 20 to 25 minutes, until the filling is bubbling and the crust is lightly browned on top.

Yield: 6 servings

CHAPTER 4

Main Courses— Meat

FLANK STEAK with WILD MUSHROOMS and HERBS

1 1/2 pounds flank steak, sliced paper thin
Salt
Freshly ground black pepper
6 shallots, peeled and minced
1/4 cup canola oil
1/2 pound fresh shiitakes, chanterelles, morels, or other wild
 mushrooms, sliced
1/2 cup beef broth
1/4 cup dry red wine
1 tablespoon tomato paste
1 teaspoon tarragon

Season the meat with salt and pepper to taste and sprinkle with the shallots. Heat a large sauté pan over medium-high heat until very hot, then add the oil. When the oil is hot, add the meat and stir-fry for 2 minutes, or until the meat loses its redness. Add the sliced mushrooms and cook for 2 minutes, stirring well. Add the broth, wine, tomato paste, and tarragon and continue to cook and stir until the sauce has thickened.

Yield: 4 servings

BACON and MUSHROOMS
with SPINACH over CREAMY POLENTA

This dish has so much flavor! You can substitute thin sliced bacon for the pancetta (Italian bacon) in this recipe. Sheri likes to use a variety of mushrooms when making this dish.

5 tablespoons canola margarine, divided
1 1/4 pounds spinach, torn into 1-inch pieces
4 cups whole milk
2 cups polenta
1/2 teaspoon salt
3/4 teaspoon freshly ground black pepper
4 ounces pancetta or bacon, coarsely chopped
4 ounces sliced crimini, oyster, or stemmed shitake mushrooms
4 tablespoons canola oil, divided
1 garlic clove, minced
1/2 cup chicken broth
2 tablespoons chopped fresh thyme
1 tablespoon lemon zest
2/3 cup freshly grated Parmesan cheese

In a medium saucepan over medium heat, melt 1 tablespoon of the margarine. Add the spinach and cook until tender, about 1 minute. Set aside.

In a large heavy saucepan over medium heat, bring the milk, 3 1/2 cups water, the polenta, and the salt and pepper to a boil, whisking constantly. Reduce the heat to low and simmer until thick, stirring constantly, about 20 minutes. Remove from heat.

In heavy large skillet over medium-high heat, cook the pancetta until it is golden brown, about 3 minutes. Transfer the pancetta to paper towels to drain.

Add the mushrooms and 2 tablespoons of the oil to the drippings remaining in the skillet. Sauté until the mushrooms are tender, about 6 minutes. Stir in the spinach and pancetta. Add garlic and broth and simmer until the broth is slightly reduced, about 6 minutes. Stir in the thyme, lemon zest, and remaining oil. Season to taste with salt and pepper. Whisk the remaining margarine and Parmesan into the polenta and divide among plates. Top with the spinach mixture.

Yield: 6 servings

BALSAMIC CANOLA GLAZE

This sauce, a combination of only two simple ingredients, makes a wonderful accompaniment to any meat dish. The Colemans especially like the tangy zest that it adds to roasted pork baked with rosemary.

1 (12-ounce) bottle high-quality balsamic vinegar
2 tablespoons canola margarine

Pour balsamic vinegar into a medium-sized saucepan and bring to a boil. Reduce the heat to maintain a slow rolling boil and reduce the volume by one-half. Remove the pan from the heat and stir in the canola margarine until it is smooth. Use immediately.
Yield: 2/3 cup

PORT SAUCE

This sauce is a variation of one that Sheri first tasted in Big Sky, Montana. By removing the saturated fat, you can enjoy this sauce over beef, pork, or game without all of the guilt.

2 cups port wine
1 cup canola margarine

Combine the ingredients in a medium saucepan over medium-low heat and bring to a slow rolling boil, stirring occasionally. Let the sauce boil slowly until the volume is reduced by one-half. Use immediately.
Yield: 1 1/2 cups

BARBECUED VEAL CHOPS
with MACADAMIA NUTS

This recipe has been adapted from one in Hugh Carpenter and Teri Sandison's *Chopstix: Quick Cooking with Pacific Flavors* (Stewart Tabori & Chang, 1997). The marinade in this recipe can alternatively be used with veal, chicken, and fish before barbecuing.

4 (10-ounce) veal chops
4 garlic cloves, finely minced
1 tablespoon finely minced ginger
1 tablespoon lemon zest
1 tablespoon orange zest
2 bunches chives, minced
1/3 cup freshly squeezed lemon juice
1/4 cup freshly squeezed orange juice
3 tablespoons dry sherry
4 tablespoons canola oil, divided
2 tablespoons Dijon mustard
2 tablespoons light soy sauce
Freshly ground black pepper
2 ounces macadamia nuts

Place the chops in a single layer in a nonreactive dish. In a small bowl, combine the garlic, ginger, lemon and orange zests, chives, lemon and orange juices, sherry, 3 tablespoons of the oil, mustard, soy sauce, and pepper to taste. Pour the marinade over the chops, cover, and refrigerate for 1 to 3 hours. Drain the meat and save the marinade.

Preheat the gas grill to 350°F (medium heat). If using charcoal or wood, prepare the fire. When coals or wood are ash covered, brush the grilling rack with the remaining oil and place the chops on the grill. Grill the veal for about 10 minutes on each side, basting with some of the reserved marinade. The veal is done when the internal temperature reaches 150°F and the meat feels firm when pressed with your fingers. Preheat the oven to 350°F. Line a cookie sheet with parchment paper. Place the macadamia nuts on the prepared pan and bake for 5 minutes or until lightly golden in color. Cool. When cool, coarsely chop the nuts. Do not use a food processor for chopping. Set the chopped nuts aside.

Place the chops on 4 dinner plates. Transfer the marinade to a small pan, bring it to a boil, and then spoon it over the chops. Sprinkle the macadamia nuts on top. Serve immediately.

Yield: 4 servings

CHINESE STEAK
with PEA PODS

This is a very satisfying, flavorful dish. It is best served over boiled rice.

1 pound flank steak
3 tablespoons hoisin sauce
2 tablespoons soy sauce
1 teaspoon sesame oil (Chinese is preferred)
2 teaspoons cornstarch
1/2 teaspoon garlic powder
3 to 4 thin slices fresh ginger, finely chopped
3/4 cup canola oil, divided
1 (10-ounce) package fresh or frozen Chinese pea pods
     (defrosted, drained, and patted dry if frozen)
1/2 pound mushrooms, thinly sliced, optional
2 firm tomatoes, cut into wedges

Slice the meat into thin strips, about 1/ 2-inch wide by 1 1/2-inches long.

In a bowl, combine the hoisin, soy sauce, sesame oil, cornstarch, garlic powder, and ginger. Add the meat to the sauce and mix well to coat each piece.

In a wok over medium heat, heat 2 to 3 tablespoons of the canola oil. Add half of the marinated meat and cook, stirring constantly, until the meat is done, about 3 minutes. Remove the meat and place on a platter. Add more oil to the wok if needed. Let the oil heat before cooking the remaining meat. Place the meat on the platter.

Add the pea pods and the mushrooms, if using, to the wok and cook, stirring, for 1 minute. Return the meat to the wok, add the tomato wedges, mix well, and cook just long enough to heat the tomatoes. Serve immediately.

Yield: 4 to 6 servings

BEEF with OYSTER SAUCE

When Sheilah's children were little, they used to go camping. While the other families dragged large pots of water to the fire and waited forever for them to boil so that they could cook their spaghetti, Sheilah took out her wok and made this dish. She was finished and cleaned up before they began to eat.

1/4 cup soy sauce
1 tablespoon sugar
1/4 cup oyster sauce, divided
2 pounds round steak, thinly sliced
4 to 5 scallions
2 teaspoons cornstarch
1/4 cup canola oil, plus additional as needed
1 tablespoon dry white sherry
1/4 teaspoon finely chopped fresh ginger, or 1/2 teaspoon ground
    ginger
2 dashes Tabasco sauce

In a shallow dish, combine the soy sauce, sugar, and 2 tablespoons of the oyster sauce. Place the meat in the marinade. Cover the dish and refrigerate for at least 1 hour.

While the meat is marinating, chop the scallions into 1/2-inch pieces, being sure to include some of the green parts. Set aside.

Remove the meat and marinade from the refrigerator and stir in the cornstarch until well blended. Heat the oil over high heat in a wok and add the marinated meat a handful at a time. Vigorously stir the meat until it is well done, 3 to 5 minutes. As the meat cooks, push it up the sides of the wok so that there is room for more meat at the bottom of the pan, near the heat. Add more oil as needed; be sure to let the fresh oil get hot before adding more meat.

When the meat is finished cooking, add the remaining 2 tablespoons of the oyster sauce, the scallions, sherry, ginger, and Tabasco sauce. Stir well and cook for another minute or two. Serve hot with cooked rice.

Yield: 4 to 6 servings

GROUND BEEF with
EGGPLANT in GARLIC SAUCE

Next time you get a yen for something Chinese, try this recipe. You can leave out the meat for a delicious vegetarian main course. Without the meat, this dish can be made ahead and served cold. This recipe has been adapted from one of Sheilah Kaufman's recipes.

2 medium eggplants, or 1 pound fresh green beans
6 garlic cloves, minced
2 to 3 tablespoons chili paste
4 tablespoons dark soy sauce
2 tablespoons black, white, or cider vinegar
2 tablespoons sugar
9 tablespoons canola oil
1/4 pound ground beef
1 1/2 cups diced scallions

Cut the eggplants into 3x3/4-inch strips but don't peel. If using beans, cut off the ends and cut the beans in half. Combine the minced garlic with the chili paste. In another bowl, mix the soy sauce, vinegar, and sugar.

Heat a wok or skillet over medium heat and add 3 tablespoons of the oil. As soon as the oil gets hot, add half of the eggplant and stir-fry until it begins to brown. Remove the vegetables to a platter and repeat with the remaining eggplant, using another 3 tablespoons oil.

Add the remaining oil to the pan, and when it is hot, add the garlic-chili paste mixture. Stir for about 12 seconds and add the ground beef. Stir until the meat is lightly browned. Return the eggplant to the pan and stir to mix well. Add the soy-vinegar mixture and stir for a minute. Serve immediately, garnished with scallions.

Yield: 4 to 6 servings

LAMB RACKS with
HERBED PINE NUT CRUST

2 cups pine nuts
4 cups flat-leaf parsley, leaves only
8 garlic cloves, crushed
1/2 cup fresh sage leaves
4 tablespoons canola oil
4 tablespoons Dijon mustard
Salt
Freshly ground black pepper
4 (13-ounce) racks of lamb, trimmed

Preheat the oven to 350°F. Line a baking pan with parchment paper. Place the pine nuts on the prepared baking pan and bake for 5 minutes or until lightly golden in color. Cool.

Coarsely chop the cooled nuts, parsley, garlic, and sage. Mix with the oil, mustard, and salt and pepper to taste. Coat the lamb with the pine nut mixture. Place the lamb in a baking dish and cook in the oven for 25 to 30 minutes, or until desired doneness.

Yield: 8 servings

LAMB WITH PRUNES

Many Sephardic main course recipes combine meat and fruit. This is from *Sephardic Israeli Cuisine* (Hippocrene Books, 2002).

4 tablespoons canola oil
2 1/2 pounds lamb, cut into 2-inch chunks
1 onion, peeled
2 bunches cilantro, tied together
1 teaspoon ground ginger
Pinch of saffron
2 teaspoons ground cinnamon
1 cinnamon stick
1 pound pitted uncooked prunes
5 to 6 tablespoons honey
1 1/2 tablespoons orange flower water
2 to 3 tablespoons white sesame seeds or blanched almonds

Place the oil, lamb chunks, whole onion, cilantro bunches, ginger, saffron, cinnamon, and cinnamon stick in a large heavy pot. Cover everything with 3 cups of water. Bring to a boil, cover, reduce heat to a simmer, and cook for 45 minutes to 1 hour, until the lamb is tender and the cooking liquid has been reduced.

Remove the onion, cinnamon stick, and cilantro bunches from the pot and discard. Turn the meat over a few times in the cooking liquid and add the prunes. Reduce the heat to a simmer, cover, and cook another 10 to 15 minutes, stirring once. If the lamb becomes too dry, add a little more water. If the sauce is too watery, remove the meat, turn the heat to high and bring it to a boil, uncovered. Cook until the sauce is reduced to about a cup of liquid. Return the meat to the pot, stir in the honey, cover the pot, reduce the heat to simmer, and cook 10 minutes. Add the orange flower water, stir and cook for a minute or two to incorporate the flavor. Adjust the seasonings if needed.

Place the lamb and prunes on a serving platter, and pour the thickened sauce over them. Sprinkle with sesame seeds and serve immediately.

Yield: 4 to 6 servings

PAKISTANI-STYLE
LAMB PATTIES

Pine nuts, oregano, garlic, and lamb combine in these savory patties for a delicious Middle East–inspired burger. This recipe is adapted from one in the Culinary Institute of America's *Grilling: Exciting International Flavors from the World's Premier Culinary College.*

6 tablespoons fresh white breadcrumbs
3 tablespoons pine nuts
2 tablespoons canola oil
3 tablespoons minced yellow onion
1 1/2 teaspoons minced garlic
2 1/2 pounds lean ground lamb
2 large eggs, lightly beaten
3 tablespoons chopped parsley
2 tablespoons tahini
2 tablespoons grated fresh ginger
2 tablespoons ground cumin
3/4 teaspoon ground coriander
3/4 teaspoon ground fennel seeds
1 1/2 teaspoons salt
3/4 teaspoon ground black pepper

Soak the breadcrumbs in 1/4 cup cold water until they are well moistened, about 2 minutes, then squeeze out any excess moisture. Place the crumbs in a bowl.

Toast the pine nuts in a small, dry skillet over medium heat, swirling the pan while the nuts cook. As they heat up they will become shiny, and then they will turn brown quickly. When the nuts are just slightly paler than you'd like, pour them out of the pan into a cool bowl.

Heat the oil in a sauté pan over medium-high heat. Add the onion and sauté, stirring frequently until translucent, 4 to 5 minutes. Add the garlic and sauté about 1 minute. Remove from heat and transfer to a plate to cool. Combine the breadcrumbs and the onion-garlic mixture with the lamb, egg, pine nuts, parsley, tahini, ginger, cumin, coriander, fennel, salt, and pepper. Mix gently until blended. Shape the mixture into 8 patties about 4 inches in diameter and 3/4 inch thick and chill them in the refrigerator.

Preheat the gas grill to medium-high, or if using a charcoal grill, let the fire burn down until the coals glow red and have a moderate coating of white ash. Grill the patties over direct heat until medium, about 4 minutes on each side, or until desired doneness.
Yield: 8 servings

LEMON HERB
GRILLED STEAK

3 tablespoons canola oil
1/4 cup freshly squeezed lemon juice
1 teaspoon liquid honey
1 tablespoon fresh rosemary
1 teaspoon chopped fresh parsley
1/4 teaspoon salt
1/4 teaspoon ground black pepper
1 pound London broil or flank steak

Combine the oil, lemon juice, honey, rosemary, parsley, salt, and pepper in a rescalable plastic bag. Add the steak and turn the bag so that the marinade coats the steak on all sides. Seal the bag and refrigerate for 12 hours or overnight.

Remove steak from the marinade, pat dry, and discard the marinade. Preheat the grill. Grill the steak over medium heat to desired doneness, about 8 minutes per side.
Yield: 4 servings

PICADILLO

This unique Spanish empanada filling has a variety of tastes and textures. It can be used in tacos or stuffed green peppers, or you can eat it plain or over rice, pasta, or matzo as a main course. This recipe is from Sheilah Kaufman's *Simply Irresistible: Easy, Elegant, Fearless, Fussless Cooking.*

3 tablespoons canola oil
2 pounds ground beef
1 cup chopped onions
1 to 2 garlic cloves, finely chopped
3 tomatoes, peeled, seeded, and coarsely chopped
2 cooking apples, peeled, cored, and coarsely chopped
1 (4-ounce) can chopped green chilies, drained, or 1 or 2 fresh
     jalapeños, seeded and chopped
2/3 cup golden raisins
10 pimento-stuffed green olives, cut in half
1/2 teaspoon ground cinnamon
1/8 teaspoon ground cloves
Salt
Freshly ground black pepper
1/2 cup blanched slivered almonds

Heat 2 tablespoons of the oil in a heavy skillet over high heat. Add the ground beef and cook, stirring constantly, breaking up any lumps in the meat. When the meat shows no sign of pink, add the onions and garlic and stir well. Reduce the heat to medium and cook for another 4 minutes. Stir in the tomatoes, apples, chilies, raisins, olives, cinnamon, cloves, and salt and pepper to taste. Simmer, uncovered, over low heat for 15 to 20 minutes, stirring occasionally.

In a small skillet heat the remaining oil over medium heat, tipping the skillet to make sure the bottom of the pan is evenly coated. Add the almonds and cook for 2 minutes or until golden brown. Be careful not to burn them. Drain the almonds well and add to the meat mixture a few minutes before serving.

Yield: 6 to 8 servings

STUFFED CABBAGE

It is believed that people in the Middle and Near East used cabbage leaves as an alternative to grape leaves in stuffing recipes. Every country from Greece to Persia to Egypt has a version of this classic. This recipe is from Sheilah Kaufman's *Sephardic Israeli Cuisine: A Mediterranean Mosaic* (Hippocrene Books, 2002).

1 large head cabbage
2 tablespoons canola oil
2 onions, sliced
1 (28-ounce) can tomatoes
3 teaspoons salt
Ground black pepper
1 or 2 beef bones with marrow
1 pound ground beef
3 tablespoons white rice, uncooked
4 tablespoons grated onion
1 large egg
3 tablespoons honey, plus additional to taste
1/4 cup freshly squeezed lemon juice
1/4 cup golden raisins

Soften cabbage by soaking the head in boiling water or by removing the core and freezing the heat overnight. Remove 12 large leaves and set aside.

Heat the oil in a deep heavy pot and lightly brown the onions. Add the tomatoes, 1 1/2 teaspoons of the salt, pepper to taste, and the bones. Cook over low heat for 30 minutes.

Combine the beef, raw rice, grated onion, egg, the remaining salt, pepper to taste, and 3 tablespoons cold water and mix well. Place some meat mixture on each cabbage leaf. Fold the sides over the filling and roll up carefully. Add the rolls to the sauce, one next to the other so that they are touching. Cover and cook over low heat for 1 1/2 hours.

Combine the honey, lemon juice, and raisins, add to the pot and cook an additional 30 minutes.

Yield: 6 main course servings or 12 first course servings

PORK and PRUNES
a la LOIRE

This unusual dish is quite rich. French bread and a green salad will suffice as accompaniments. The prunes need to be soaked overnight, so start this recipe the day before serving.

30 prunes, pitted
2 cups white wine (Vouvray is preferred)
3 pounds boneless pork tenderloin
1/3 cup flour
3 tablespoons canola margarine or butter
3 tablespoons canola oil
Salt
Freshly ground black pepper
1 tablespoon red currant jelly
1 cup whipping cream

The day before serving, place the prunes in a small glass bowl, and pour the wine over them. Cover and refrigerate overnight.

The next day, transfer the prunes and wine to a small saucepan. Cook them over low heat for about 30 minutes, or until the prunes are soft. Drain the prunes, reserving the wine for the sauce, and set aside.

Cut the pork into 1/2-inch-thick slices and remove any excess fat. Place the flour on a plate and dredge the slices lightly, shaking off any excess flour.

Preheat oven to 200 to 250°F.

In a large skillet over medium heat, heat the margarine and oil and sauté the pork slices. Do not crowd the pieces in the skillet. Brown the pork slowly on both sides; then cook gently until the meat is tender, about 20 minutes. Season the meat with salt and pepper to taste.

Transfer the slices to a shallow ovenproof baking dish. Let the slices overlap slightly. Arrange a row of prunes on each side of the pork slices. Cover the baking dish with foil and place in the oven to keep the meat warm while you make the sauce.

To make the sauce, add the reserved wine to the skillet and, with a wire whisk, scrape up any pieces of flour and meat that have stuck to the pan. This is called deglazing. Add the jelly and continue to stir and cook until the jelly is dissolved and blended into the sauce. Cook the sauce for a few minutes over medium-low heat to reduce it slightly. Bring the sauce to a boil, stirring constantly. Remove the skillet from the heat, and whisk in 1/2 cup of the cream. Return the skillet to the heat again and add as much of the remaining cream as needed to make a sauce that will coat a wooden spoon. The more cream you add, the less flavor the sauce will have; however, it should not be too thick.

Pour the sauce over the meat and prunes and serve at once.

Yield: 4 to 6 servings

MARINATED FLANK STEAK

1 1/2 pounds flank steak
3/4 cup canola oil
1/4 cup soy sauce
1/4 cup honey
2 tablespoons cider vinegar
2 tablespoons minced scallions
1 to 2 garlic cloves, minced
1 teaspoon ground ginger

Score the meat on both sides. In a shallow bowl, combine the oil, soy sauce, honey, vinegar, scallions, garlic, and ginger. Add the meat to the marinade and turn to coat on all sides. Cover the dish and refrigerate for 4 hours.

Remove the meat from the refrigerator and discard the marinade. The meat may be grilled or broiled; cook about 5 minutes per side for medium rare. Carve the meat on the diagonal, across the grain, in thin slices.

Yield: 4 to 6 servings

SATAY

Satay is an exotic Indonesian dish that is sure to win raves. This dish doubles as an appetizer, and satay sauce, at room temperature, can be used as an unusual dressing for any vegetable salad.

The sauce:
1 large onion, grated
2 garlic cloves, minced
1 tablespoon chili powder
1 tablespoon canola oil
2 teaspoons ground coriander
1 teaspoon ground cumin
6 tablespoons chunky peanut butter
1 1/2 cups coconut milk (not juice)
3 tablespoons brown sugar, packed
2 tablespoons soy sauce
2 tablespoons freshly squeezed lemon juice

The skewers:
1 pound beef, cut into 1/2-inch strips
2 whole chicken breasts, skinned, boned, and cut into small
     pieces
1/4 cup soy sauce (approximately)
1/4 cup dry sherry (approximately)

In a large saucepan, combine the onion, garlic, chili powder, and oil. Cook over medium heat, stirring, for 2 minutes. Add the coriander and cumin and cook and stir for another 5 minutes. Add the peanut butter, coconut milk, brown sugar, soy sauce, and lemon juice. Stir well to mix and simmer until thickened. Set aside.

Preheat the oven to broil.

If using wooden skewers, soak the skewers in a bowl of water for about 20 minutes.

Thread the beef and chicken alternately on 8 to 12 bamboo skewers. Lay the skewers on a cake rack over a shallow ovenproof baking dish. Sprinkle the beef and chicken with equal parts of the soy sauce and sherry, coating each piece. Broil the meat 6 inches from the heat for 3 to 5 minutes, turning once.

While the meat is broiling, gently reheat the sauce. Transfer the sauce to a bowl and serve along with the skewers, for dipping.
Yield: 8 to 12 servings

SOUTHWESTERN-STYLE QUICHE

1 recipe for Piecrust (made with canola oil), unbaked (see page 213)
2 tablespoons canola oil
1 cup corn
1/2 cup red bell pepper
1/4 cup green bell pepper
1 tablespoon finely chopped red onion
Pinch of salt
Ground black pepper
1/4 teaspoon dried oregano
3/4 cup grated cheddar cheese
3/4 cup cooked bacon
4 large eggs
1 1/4 cups milk
1 tablespoon fresh parsley, or 1 teaspoon dried
1/8 teaspoon ground nutmeg

Preheat the oven to 375°F. Place the piecrust in a pie pan and cover the crust with foil. Place pie weights on top of the foil and bake for about 15 minutes, or until golden brown. Transfer to a wire rack, remove the weights and the foil and let cool.

In large skillet, heat the oil over medium-high heat and add the corn, red pepper, green pepper, and onion. Season with the salt, pepper to taste, and the oregano. Sauté until cooked, stirring frequently, for about 8 minutes. Set aside.

Add 1/2 cup of the cheddar cheese to the baked piecrust. Add the vegetables and bacon. In a large bowl, whisk together the eggs, milk, parsley, and nutmeg. Pour the egg mixture into the pie plate and sprinkle the remaining cheese on top. Bake the quiche for 30 to 35 minutes. Let stand for 5 minutes and serve.
Yield: 6 servings

Hint: Dry rice or beans can be used as an alternative to pie weights.

TOSTADAS MEXICANO

These open-faced sandwiches remind me of a snowcapped Mexican mountain.

1 large head iceberg lettuce, thinly sliced
1 bunch scallions, chopped (white with 1 inch of the green)
1/2 pound Monterey Jack cheese, grated
1 pound chorizo
1 (15- to 16-ounce) can Mexican-style refried beans
1/4 to 1/2 cup canola oil
4 (8- to 10-inch) flour tortillas
1 cup medium-mild red taco sauce
4 tomatoes, cut in wedges, for garnish
avocado wedges for garnish
chopped ripe olives for garnish
turkey or chicken, sliced and cut into julienne, for garnish
1 to 2 pints sour cream for garnish
Paprika for garnish

About 30 minutes before you begin, chill a large bowl in the refrigerator.

Combine the lettuce, scallions, and cheese in the prepared bowl. Cover and refrigerate.

Remove the chorizo from its casing, and in a large skillet, cook the meat until it is brown and crumbly. Add the beans and cook, stirring, for 2 to 3 minutes to heat the beans through. Remove the mixture from the heat, cover, and keep warm.

Preheat the oven to 140°F. Heat 4 large plates in the oven for serving.

In another skillet, heat about 1/2-inch of oil until it is very hot, and fry the tortillas, one at a time, until they are golden-brown and crisp. Remove the tortillas from the oil and drain well on paper towels. Transfer the tortillas to the plates in the oven if not serving right away. To serve, remove the tortillas and the plates from the oven and spread equal amounts of the chorizo-bean mixture over each one. Toss the lettuce, scallion, and cheese with the taco sauce, and heap this mixture on top of the chorizo-bean mixture. Arrange the optional garnish ingredients on each side of the "mountain" and top with sour cream to taste, letting the cream run down the mountain's sides. Finish with a flourish of paprika.

Yield: 4 servings

YANKEE POT ROAST

According to my friend Ginny, a food writer, this venerable recipe has become a staple of classic American cookery. Pot roast is traditionally cooked slowly in a tightly covered kettle or pot with a fair amount of wine or broth, but it can also be prepared in the oven or in a slow cooker. Any way you choose to prepare the roast, be sure you keep plenty of liquid in the pot to tenderize the meat. Slow cooking allows you to select a more economical cut of beef.

4 pounds boneless beef roast
Salt
Freshly ground black pepper
1/4 cup flour
1/4 cup canola oil
1 bay leaf
1 sprig of parsley
1 tablespoon golden raisins
6 carrots, peeled and sliced
6 onions, thinly sliced
1 white turnip, sliced
6 potatoes, peeled and quartered

Rub the meat all over with salt and pepper to taste, and then rub it all over with the flour.

Bring a pot of water to a boil.

Heat the canola oil in a large, heavy kettle over high heat, and brown the meat on all sides. Use a large spoon or tongs to turn meat, being careful not to pierce it. When the meat is a rich brown on all sides, add enough of the boiling water to cover the bottom of kettle. Add the bay leaf, parsley, and raisins. Cover and simmer over low heat for 3 hours, adding more water if necessary. Add the carrots, onions, and turnip and simmer for 30 minutes. Then add the potatoes and cook 30 minutes more.

To serve, discard the bay leaf and parsley. Remove the meat and vegetables to a platter with a slotted spoon. If desired, thicken the gravy with a mixture of 2 tablespoons flour and 1/4 cup water.
Yield: 6 to 8 servings

CHAPTER 5

Main Courses— Meatless

BLACK BEAN CHILI

If you cook this until it gets really thick, it can also be used as a dip. This is from Sheilah Kaufman's *Simply Irresistible: Easy, Elegant, Fearless, Fussless Cooking.*

2 tablespoons canola oil
1 medium onion, chopped
1 red pepper, stemmed, seeded, and diced
Salt
Freshly ground black pepper
1 teaspoon dried oregano
1 teaspoon dried cumin
1 (15-ounce) can diced tomatoes
1 (4-ounce) can chopped mild green chilies
4 garlic cloves, minced
2 (14-ounce) cans black beans, drained and rinsed
1/2 cup grated cheddar cheese, optional

Heat the oil in a large pot over medium heat. Sauté the onion and red pepper for about 5 minutes. Reduce the heat to medium-low and stir in salt and pepper to taste, the oregano, the cumin, and the tomatoes. Cook for about 5 minutes. Add the chopped green chilies and garlic. Mix well and continue cooking for another 10 to 15 minutes. Stir in the black beans. Continue cooking and stirring occasionally for another 20 to 30 minutes. Sprinkle with cheese if desired and serve hot over rice.

Yield: 6 servings

BELL PEPPER STIR-FRY

The sauce:

1 (14-ounce) can pineapple chucks, drained and juice reserved
2 teaspoons honey
3 tablespoons soy sauce
1/3 cup brown sugar, packed
3 tablespoons white vinegar
3 teaspoons cornstarch
Dash of ground cloves
Dash of ground cinnamon

The stir-fry:

2 tablespoons canola oil
2 garlic cloves, crushed
2 teaspoons fresh ginger, grated
1/2 yellow bell pepper, sliced
1/2 red bell pepper, sliced
1/2 orange bell pepper, sliced
1/2 cup snow peas, washed and ends removed
1 (14-ounce) can baby corn, drained
1 (10-ounce) can water chestnuts, drained
1 apple, diced and drizzled with lemon juice to preserve color
1/2 cup dried cranberries, rinsed
1/2 head Chinese celery cabbage, chopped
6 cups cooked rice noodles

To prepare the sauce, drain the juice from the can of pineapples over a bowl. Set the pineapples aside. Whisk the honey, soy sauce, sugar, vinegar, 1/4 cup water, cornstarch, ground cloves, and cinnamon into the pineapple juice. Set aside.

In a nonstick wok or skillet, heat the oil. Add the garlic and ginger and stir and heat for 30 seconds. Add the peppers, snow peas, baby corn, water chestnuts, apple, reserved pineapple, and cranberries. Stir-fry the vegetables until crisp but heated thoroughly, 3 to 4 minutes. Add the sauce, mix well, and heat until the sauce thickens. Turn the heat down and add the celery cabbage. Stir.

Remove the vegetables from the heat and serve immediately on a bed of noodles.

Yield: 6 servings

BREAD CUP EGGS

These bread cups are large croustades. This easy recipe is a great way to serve eggs to company. The Coleman family loves these on a Saturday morning with fresh squeezed orange juice and fresh sliced bananas.

Canola oil for greasing
12 slices bread, crusts removed
1 (4-ounce) stick canola margarine, melted, plus additional as
    needed
12 small eggs

Preheat oven to 350°F. Grease a 12-cup muffin tin and gently press the bread into the prepared muffin cups. Brush inside of each slice of bread with melted margarine and cook in the oven until slighty browned. Break a small egg into each bread cup and bake for 10 minutes or until the egg is set.
Yield: 6 servings

EGG SOUFFLE

This wonderful recipe is courtesy of Sheilah's friend Elliot, the caterer.

4 tablespoons canola margarine, plus additional for greasing
1 green bell pepper, seeded and chopped
1 onion, chopped
1/2 to 1 pound mushrooms, thinly sliced
12 large eggs
1/2 cup flour
1 teaspoon baking powder
1/2 teaspoon salt
1 pint small curd creamed cottage cheese
1 pound grated cheddar cheese
1/2 cup melted canola margarine
3 tomatoes, thinly sliced

Preheat the oven to 350°F. Grease a 9x13-inch baking dish with canola margarine.

In a large skillet over medium heat, melt the margarine in a large skillet and sauté the green pepper, onion, and mushrooms. Drain the vegetables well.

Beat eggs well and add flour, baking powder, and salt. Slowly blend in the cheeses, sautéed vegetables, and melted margarine. Place in the prepared baking dish. Top with the tomatoes. Bake for 45 minutes to 1 hour and 15 minutes, or until set and golden brown.

Yield: 15 servings

FRESH TOMATO TART

This tart is another of Sherron Goldstein's winners.

1 recipe Piecrust (made with canola oil), unbaked (see page 213)
1 1/2 cups grated mozzarella cheese
1 1/2 cups grated Swiss cheese
1 cup thinly sliced fresh basil, divided
4 large tomatoes, peeled, seeded, and cut into 1/4-inch slices
2 tablespoons canola oil
Salt
Ground black pepper

Preheat the oven to 400°F. Lay the piecrust in a pie pan, trim the edges if necessary, and prick the bottom and sides of the pastry. Bake without the filling according to package directions.

In a bowl, combine the cheeses. When the crust has finished cooking, sprinkle half of the cheese evenly over the bottom of the crust. Sprinkle 1/2 cup of the basil over the cheese. Arrange the tomato slices in circles over the basil until all are used. Brush the tomatoes with oil and season with salt and pepper to taste. Sprinkle the remaining basil over the tomatoes and top with the remaining cheese. Bake for 8 to 10 minutes.

Yield: 8 servings

EGGPLANT and
CHICKPEA TAGINE

Tagine is best with fresh, seasonal ingredients from local growers. This recipe, perfect for entertaining, is from Sherron Goldstein's *Fresh Fields: Entertaining with Southern Comfort.*

1 large eggplant, cut into 1/2-inch dice
2 zucchini, thinly sliced
1/3 cup canola oil, divided
Salt
Freshly ground black pepper
1 1/2 cups sliced onions
6 garlic cloves, chopped
2 cups crimini mushrooms, cut in half
1 1/2 tablespoons ground coriander
2 teaspoons cumin seeds
1 1/2 tablespoons ground cinnamon
2 teaspoons ground turmeric
2 cups red potatoes, quartered
2 1/2 cups vegetable broth
2 tablespoons tomato paste
2 tablespoons chili sauce
1/2 cup dried apricots
3 cups drained canned chickpeas
1/4 cup chopped fresh cilantro, for garnish

Preheat the oven to 425°F. Toss the eggplant and zucchini in a bowl with 4 tablespoons of the oil, and add salt and pepper to taste. Arrange the eggplant and zucchini on a baking sheet, and bake for 20 minutes, turning occasionally. Do not over-brown.

Heat the remaining 4 teaspoons oil in a large sauté pan. Cook the onion and garlic until the garlic turns a light golden color. Add the mushrooms and sauté an additional 3 to 5 minutes until tender. Add the coriander, cumin seeds, cinnamon, and turmeric. Mix well and cook for another minute. Add the potatoes and sauté 3 minutes. Pour in the vegetable broth and tomato paste, cover, and cook for 10 minutes at a medium simmer. The sauce should begin to thicken. Add the eggplant, zucchini, chili sauce, apricots, and chickpeas. Season with salt and pepper to taste. Partially cover and cook for an additional 15

to 20 minutes. If tagine becomes too dry, add more broth. Sprinkle with cilantro to serve.
Yield: 6 servings

GRILLED STUFFED PORTOBELLO MUSHROOMS

Warm portobello mushroom caps oozing with herbed goat cheese and sun-dried tomatoes are delectable paired with a simple green salad. Or cut these treats into wedges and serve as an appetizer. This recipe is from Cathy Thomas and Nick Koon's *Melissa's Great Book of Produce: Everything You Need to Know about Fresh Fruits and Vegetables* (Wiley, 2006).

2/3 cup drained marinated sun-dried tomatoes, chopped
1/4 cup soft goat cheese
1 teaspoon canola oil, divided
1/2 teaspoon chopped fresh rosemary
1/8 teaspoon ground black pepper
1 garlic clove, minced
4 portobello mushroom caps, 5 to 6 inches in diameter
2 tablespoons freshly squeezed lemon juice
2 teaspoons low-sodium soy sauce
2 teaspoons chopped fresh cilantro or Italian parsley, for garnish

Prepare the grill.

In a small bowl, combine the tomatoes, the goat cheese, 1/2 teaspoon of the oil, the rosemary, the pepper, and the garlic. Stir to combine well.

Remove the mushroom stems from the caps. Using a spoon, scoop out the dark gills and discard.

In a small bowl, mix the remaining oil, the lemon juice, and the soy sauce. Using a pastry brush, brush the soy sauce mixture on both sides of the mushroom caps. Grill the caps stem-side down about 5 minutes. Turn and grill until soft, about 5 minutes more.

Spoon 1/4 cup of the cheese mixture into each cap. Cover the grill and grill the stuffed caps for about 3 minutes or until the cheese melts. Garnish with cilantro and serve.
Yield: 4 servings

GROWN-UP MACARONI
and CHEESE

This dish is the ultimate comfort food! I borrowed this recipe from Sherron Goldstein's *Fresh Fields: Entertaining with Southern Comfort.*

Canola spray for greasing
4 tablespoons canola oil
1 large onion, chopped
6 garlic cloves, thinly sliced
1 pound fusilli pasta
1 (32-ounce) can crushed tomatoes in tomato sauce
2 cups grated Swiss cheese, plus extra for topping
1 cup grated Parmesan cheese, plus extra for topping
1 cup grated cheddar cheese, plus extra for topping
1/2 cup half-and-half
1 tablespoon dried oregano
1 tablespoon dried marjoram
Salt
Ground black pepper

Preheat the oven to 350°F. Grease a baking dish with the spray.

In a large skillet, heat the oil over medium heat and sauté the onion and garlic. Cook until the onions are transparent and the garlic is just turning golden. Remove from heat and set aside.

Cook the pasta in a large pot according to the directions on the package. Drain but do not rinse.

Place the pasta in a large bowl. Add the onions and garlic and toss to mix well. Add the tomatoes and sauce, cheeses, half-and-half, oregano, marjoram, and salt and pepper to taste. Toss all of the ingredients together.

Transfer the pasta to the prepared baking dish. Sprinkle with a few tablespoons of each additional cheese and bake for 45 to 60 minutes. The top of the casserole should be just starting to brown when you remove it from the oven. Let it cool a few minutes before serving.
Yield: 8 servings

ROASTED PUMPKIN and
SPINACH PENNE

Whenever guests arrive at Sherron Goldstein's house the first thing they notice are the wonderful aromas of food cooking! This marvelous fall and winter dish has been adapted from one in Goldstein's *Fresh Fields: Entertaining with Southern Comfort.* Roasted cherry tomatoes may be added for their lovely taste and color.

Canola oil spray for greasing
3 pounds pie pumpkin, peeled and cubed
6 tablespoons canola oil
Salt
Freshly ground black pepper
1 (1-pound) package penne
12 ounces fresh baby spinach, washed and torn into pieces
1 teaspoon grated fresh nutmeg
4 tablespoons canola margarine
4 tablespoons fresh sage leaves
1/4 cup lemon zest
2 tablespoons freshly squeezed lemon juice
1/2 cup slivered almonds, toasted

Preheat the oven to 375°F. Grease a 9x13-inch baking dish with the spray. Toss the pumpkin with 2 tablespoons of the oil and place in the prepared pan. Add salt and pepper to taste and roast for 40 minutes, or until the pumpkin is browned on the edges. Set aside.

Cook the pasta in a large pot of boiling water until al dente. Drain, but do not rinse, and toss with fresh spinach and nutmeg. Cover and keep warm.

Place the margarine and the remaining oil in a pan over medium-low heat and stir until the margarine is melted. Add the sage and lemon zest and cook for one minute or until crispy.

To serve, toss the pasta-spinach mixture with the pumpkin, lemon juice, toasted almonds, sage and lemon zest mixture, and salt and pepper to taste.

Yield: 8 servings

MOUSSAKA

This easy, fabulous version of moussaka is courtesy of Shelley Sackett, owner of Kitchen Affairs in Evansville, Indiana. Shelley prefers to use male eggplants because they are more dense, have more flesh, and have fewer seeds than females, which are softer. The fewer seeds the eggplant has, the less bitter it will be. To determine if an eggplant is male or female, look at the blossom end: if it has a round mark it's male; if the mark is oval—slightly elongated—it's female. But even experts disagree on which eggplants to select. The bottom line is choose fully colored fruit with firm unwrinkled skin that feels heavy for its size and discard any parts that are darkly colored or bruised because these will more your dish taste bitter.

Baking time for this recipe will depend on how deep your casserole dish is and how well you drained the eggplant. Shelley recommends allowing about an hour and a quarter for cooking, but if the dish is done sooner, cover it loosely with foil and turn the oven back to 200°F so that the top doesn't get too brown and the dish remains warm until you are ready to serve it. Like a custard, moussaka needs to set.

1 large eggplant
1 cup milk
2 large eggs
2 teaspoons dried oregano, divided
1/2 teaspoon garlic powder, divided
3/4 cup flour for dredging
Salt
Freshly ground black pepper
Canola oil for frying
1 (14-ounce) can whole, peeled tomatoes, drained well
2 (14-ounce) cans tomato sauce
1 large onion, chopped
1 cup grated Parmesan cheese

Slice the eggplant into 3/4-inch slices. Soak the slices in heavily salted water for at least 30 minutes or up to several hours, and drain well.

Preheat the oven to 350°F.

In a bowl combine the milk, eggs, 1 teaspoon of the oregano, and 1/4 teaspoon of the garlic powder. In another bowl, place the flour, salt, pepper, and the remaining oregano and garlic powder. Dip the eggplant slices into the milk mixture and then into the seasoned flour.

In a large skillet, heat enough oil to cover the bottom of the pan. Fry the eggplant, just until brown. Drain the fried eggplant slices on a paper towel and then place them into a glass or metal baking dish in a single layer. Add the cans of tomatoes and the tomato sauce to the remaining egg-milk mixture and mix well. Sprinkle the chopped onion over the eggplant slices and top with 1/2 cup of the Parmesan cheese. Pour the tomato-milk mixture over the top, and cover with the remaining cheese.

Bake the moussaka for 45 to 90 minutes, or until the top is browned and the liquid has set and is no longer runny. Serve hot.

Yield: 8 servings

MUSHROOM and SPINACH CASSEROLE

By subbing skim and nonfat dairy products, this mushroom, spinach, and cheese dish can be made low fat. This recipe was adapted from one in Sherron Goldstein's *Fresh Fields: Entertaining with Southern Comfort*.

Canola oil spray for greasing
2 tablespoons canola margarine, melted
2 tablespoons canola oil
1 large red onion, thinly sliced
3 tablespoons garlic, chopped
2 pounds mixed fresh mushrooms, washed and sliced
2 tablespoons fresh rosemary, crushed
1/2 pound fresh baby spinach, washed and coarsely chopped
1 cup ricotta
1/2 cup milk
1 cup half-and-half
1 cup sour cream
6 large eggs, beaten, or 1 1/2 cups egg substitute
Salt
Ground black pepper
1 (8-ounce) package macaroni, cooked
1 cup grated Parmesan cheese
1/2 cup toasted breadcrumbs

Preheat the oven to 350°F. Grease a 13x9-inch pan with the spray. In a medium sauté pan, melt the margarine with the oil. Add the onion and garlic and cook over medium heat until the garlic is golden brown. Add the mushrooms and rosemary. Sauté until the mushrooms are wilted. Mix in the spinach and cook an additional 1 to 2 minutes until the spinach is also wilted. Drain if needed. Remove the vegetables from the heat and reserve.

Place the ricotta, milk, half-and-half, sour cream, and eggs in a large bowl. Beat with an electric mixer until smooth. Fold the mushroom and spinach mixture into the smooth cheese filling and add salt and pepper to taste. Add the cooked macaroni and Parmesan cheese and toss well. Spoon into the prepared pan.

Sprinkle the toasted breadcrumbs over the top of the casserole.

Bake, uncovered, for about 35 to 45 minutes, until the top of the casserole is golden brown.

Yield: 10 servings

RUSTIC PASTA with TOMATOES, OLIVES, and RICOTTA

This Old World pasta recipe has half as much saturated fat as the original because canola oil has been substituted for the olive oil. Still, the flavors in this dish really carry through. If you feel that you want that olive oil flavor, top the pasta with a small drizzle just prior to serving.

Salt
8 ounces fusilli or penne pasta
Canola oil for drizzling
10 sun-dried tomatoes in oil, drained
1 tablespoon red wine vinegar
2 teaspoons capers
2 garlic cloves, coarsely chopped
1/2 cup canola oil
Freshly ground black pepper
1/2 cup grape tomatoes, quartered
1/3 cup Kalamata olives, pitted and halved
1/3 cup fresh basil, torn
Fresh ricotta cheese, for serving

Bring a pot of salted water to a boil over high heat. Add the pasta, reduce the heat to medium high, and cook until al dente. Drain the pasta and drizzle with just enough canola oil to coat. Spread the pasta on a baking sheet and refrigerate for 10 minutes.

Place the sun-dried tomatoes, vinegar, capers, and garlic in a food processor and pulse to combine. With the machine running, add the canola oil in a slow, steady stream and process until smooth. Season with salt and pepper to taste.

Toss together the pasta, sun-dried tomato vinaigrette, tomatoes, olives, and basil. Transfer to serving plates. Top each with a scoop of ricotta, drizzle with olive oil, if desired, and sprinkle with pepper to taste.

Yield: 4 servings

SPINACH, RICE,
and FETA PIE

This fabulous dish for entertaining is courtesy of Kerry Dunnington. It can also be served in smaller portions as an appetizer or side dish.

1 cup chopped onion
2 garlic cloves, minced
1 to 2 tablespoons canola oil
1 1/4 cups milk
1/4 cup sour cream
1/2 teaspoon salt
1/4 teaspoon pepper
3 cups cooked Basmati, Jasmati, or Texmati rice
3/4 cup crumbled feta cheese
2 large eggs, lightly beaten
1 (16-ounce) bag frozen chopped spinach, thawed, or 1 large
    bunch fresh spinach, cooked, chopped, and drained of
    excess liquid
3 tablespoons grated Parmesan cheese

Preheat the oven to 400°F. Sauté the onion and garlic in oil over medium heat until soft. Transfer to a large bowl, and whisk in the milk, sour cream, salt, and pepper. Stir in the rice, feta cheese, eggs, and spinach and spoon the mixture into a 10-inch baking dish that has been coated with oil. Top the pie with Parmesan cheese. Bake for 35 to 40 minutes or until light brown and bubbly.

Yield: 6 servings

TOFU CHILI

This recipe is adapted from one in Rise' Routenberg and Barbara Wasser's *Divine Kosher Cuisine: Catering to Family and Friends* (Divine Kosher Cuisine, 2006). A nonstick pan works best when browning tofu.

1/4 cup canola oil
1 pound firm tofu, drained and mashed
1 large onion, chopped
8 ounces mushrooms, sliced
3 garlic cloves, minced
1 (15-ounce) can kidney beans, rinsed and drained
2 cups corn
2 teaspoons chili powder
1 teaspoon ground cumin
2 cups tomato sauce
Salt
Freshly ground black pepper
Tabasco or other hot pepper sauce
1/4 cup grated or shredded cheddar cheese
Tortilla chips

In a large pot, heat the oil and brown the tofu. Add the onions and mushrooms and sauté until the onions are soft. Add the garlic and sauté another 2 minutes. Mix well. Stir in the beans, corn, chili powder, cumin, tomato sauce, and salt, pepper, and hot pepper sauce to taste. Mix well, bring to a boil, reduce the heat, and simmer for 10 minutes. Spoon into bowls and top with the cheese and tortilla chips before serving.

Yield: 4 servings

TOM DOUGLAS'S
FABULOUS POTATO LATKES
with LEMON DILL CREAM

There's nothing better than a crisp golden potato latke! Try these for brunch, or omit the lemon dill cream and serve them as a side dish with pan-roasted salmon or charcoal-grilled steak. If you are headed for Seattle, check out Tom's famous restaurants: Etta's, Dahlia Lounge, Lola, and Palace Kitchen. His books include *Tom Douglas' Seattle Kitchen*, *Tom's Big Dinners*, and *I Love Crab Cakes*.

The lemon dill cream:

1 cup sour cream
1/2 cup finely chopped fresh dill
1 tablespoon freshly squeezed lemon juice
1 teaspoon lemon zest
Kosher salt
Ground black pepper

The latkes:

1 1/2 pounds large Yukon gold or russet potatoes, peeled
1 small (about 6 ounces) onion, peeled
3 large eggs, lightly beaten
4 tablespoons plus 2 teaspoons dried, plain breadcrumbs (recipe
    follows)
1 1/2 teaspoons kosher salt
3/4 teaspoon ground black pepper
Canola oil for frying

To make the cream, combine the sour cream, dill, and lemon juice and zest in a small bowl. Season to taste with salt and pepper. Store in the refrigerator until ready to serve; makes 1 1/4 cups.

To make the latkes, preheat the oven to 200°F.

Grate the potatoes and the onion using a box grater or the medium grating blade of a food processor. Lay a large piece of cheesecloth or a clean dishcloth in a large bowl, and pour in the potato-onion mixture. Gather up the edges of the cloth, forcing the grated vegetables into a tight bundle, and wring out as much liquid as you can. Discard the liquid.

Shake the potatoes and onions into a large bowl. Stir in the eggs, breadcrumbs, salt, and pepper and mix well. Using a 1/2-cup measuring cup, scoop up a portion of the batter and pat it between your hands into a pancake shape, 1/2-inch thick and 3- to 4-inches wide. Repeat until all of the latkes are shaped, placing them on a plate as you go.

Place two large nonstick or cast-iron skillets over medium-high heat and pour in enough oil to coat the bottoms of the pans (about 1/8 inch oil). When the pans are hot, add as many latkes as will comfortably fit into each pan. (To protect your hands from the hot oil, slip the latkes into the pan using a large spoon.) Fry the cakes until golden, turning with a spatula to brown both sides, about 5 minutes per side. Turn the heat down to medium as needed so the latkes don't burn before they've cooked through. Transfer the latkes to a paper towel-lined baking sheet and keep them warm in the oven as you continue to fry the remaining latkes. Be sure to wipe out any burned bits of debris from the pan and add more oil as needed. When all the latkes are fried, transfer them to plates and serve with the lemon dill cream.

Yield: 10 latkes or 4 servings

Dried Breadcrumbs

A half loaf (12 ounces or 8 slices) European-style white bread

Preheat the oven to 325°F. Cut the crust off the bread and discard. Slice the bread into 1/2-inch-thick slices. Place the slices in a single layer on an ungreased baking sheet. Put the baking sheet in the oven and bake until the bread feels dried out in the center, about 40 minutes. Turn the bread over from time to time so it dries out evenly.

Remove the bread from the oven and allow it to cool. Tear the bread into pieces and place in a food processor. Pulse until the crumbs are very fine. Sieve the crumbs to remove any large pieces. Dried breadcrumbs will keep a week or more at room temperature in a tightly sealed container. They can also be sealed in plastic bags and frozen for a month or more.

Yield: 2 1/2 cups

CHAPTER 6

Main Courses— Fish

OVEN-SEARED MARINATED SALMON

This quick but elegant salmon dish is adapted from a recipe in Sherron Goldstein's *Fresh Fields: Entertaining with Southern Comfort.*

1 cup Dijon mustard
1 cup mixed fresh chives, parsley, thyme, and sage, chopped
Salt
Freshly ground black pepper
6 (6-ounce) salmon fillets or steaks
1/2 cup canola oil
Canola oil spray for greasing

In a shallow dish, combine the mustard, herbs, and salt and pepper to taste. Place the salmon pieces in the mustard mixture and turn to coat on all sides. Using a pastry brush, seal the mustard coating with a light layer of canola oil. Cover the dish and refrigerate for at least 2 hours.

Preheat the oven to 400°F. Grease a shallow ovenproof baking dish with the spray. Place the chilled salmon in the prepared dish and bake for 12 to 15 minutes, or until the salmon flakes easily with a fork.
Yield: 6 servings

BAKED GROUPER FILLET
with ROASTED TOMATOES

This recipe was adapted from one in Sherron Goldstein's *Fresh Fields: Entertaining with Southern Comfort*. If you don't want to use grouper, try this with a similar white fish.

The fish:

4 ounces garlic, finely chopped
2 ounces fresh mint, coarsely chopped
2 ounces fresh basil, coarsely chopped
1 ounce fresh oregano, coarsely chopped
4 ounces canola oil
Salt
Freshly ground black pepper
Juice of 4 lemons
6 (4-ounce) grouper fillets

The tomatoes:

4 ounces canola oil, or less
4 ounces shallots, finely chopped
2 ounces garlic, chopped
8 large tomatoes, peeled, seeded, and diced
3 tablespoons fresh basil, cut into julienne
2 tablespoons tomato paste or ketchup
Salt
Freshly ground black pepper

In a shallow dish, combine the garlic, mint, basil, oregano, oil, salt and pepper to taste, and lemon juice. Place the fish in the marinade and turn to coat on all sides. Cover the dish and refrigerate overnight.

Preheat the oven to 375°F. For the tomatoes, heat the oil in a large skillet and sauté the shallots and garlic, just until the garlic begins to turn a light golden color. Stir in the diced tomatoes and cook for 4 to 5 minutes. Add the basil, tomato paste, and salt and pepper to taste and lightly toss until the ingredients are warm and fragrant.

Place the marinated fish in an ovenproof dish and bake for 10 to 15 minutes. Test to make sure the fish is done; it should flake easily with a fork. If fillets are more than 1 1/2 inches thick they will need to cook a little longer. To serve, divide the cooked tomatoes among six plates

and top each with a fish fillet.
Yield: 6 servings

Hint: To keep fish from sticking to a baking pan, bake on a bed of chopped onion, celery, and parsley. This also adds a nice flavor to the fish.

BLACKENED TUNA

If you love Cajun food or fish with a little zest, this dish is for you.

1 1/2 pounds fresh 1-inch-thick tuna steaks
2 tablespoons Cajun seasoning
2 tablespoons canola oil
2 tablespoons canola margarine

Generously coat the tuna with Cajun seasoning. Heat the oil and margarine in a large skillet over high heat. When the oil is nearly smoking, place the steaks in the pan. Cook on one side for 3 to 4 minutes, or until blackened. Turn the steaks and cook for 3 to 4 minutes, or to desired doneness.
Yield: 6 servings

FISH TACOS

This is a great recipe that Sheri had for the first time with her friend Jeff at a little restaurant along the boardwalk in San Diego. She went home and made the dish as close to what she had tasted as she could. Of course this recipe is full of wonderful ingredients and tastes so fresh, but in addition, when she makes it, she gets to smile and think about what a great friend she has in Jeff.

1 cup flour, plus additional for dusting
2 tablespoons cornstarch
1 teaspoon baking powder
1/2 teaspoon salt
1 egg
1 cup beer
1/2 cup plain yogurt
1/2 cup canola oil–based mayonnaise
Freshly squeezed juice of 1 lime
1 jalapeño pepper, minced
1 teaspoon minced capers
2 tablespoons fresh cilantro, chopped
1/2 teaspoon ground cumin
1 teaspoon fresh dill weed, finely chopped
1 teaspoon ground cayenne pepper
1 quart canola oil for frying
1 pound cod fillets, cut into 2- to 3-ounce portions
1 (12-ounce) package corn tortillas
1/2 medium head cabbage, finely shredded
Lime wedges

In a large bowl, combine the flour, cornstarch, baking powder, and salt. In a separate bowl, combine the egg and beer. Quickly stir the egg mixture into the flour mixture.

In a medium bowl, mix together the yogurt and mayonnaise. Gradually stir in the lime juice until the consistency is slightly runny. Stir in the jalapeño, capers, cilantro, cumin, dill, and cayenne.

Heat the oil in a deep-fryer to 375°F. Dust the fish pieces lightly with flour. Dip them into the beer batter and then fry them in the deep-fryer until crisp and golden brown. Drain on paper towels.

Lightly fry the tortillas; they should not be too crisp.

To serve, place the fried fish in a tortilla and top with the shredded cabbage and yogurt. Garnish with lime wedges.
Yield: 6 servings

GRILLED TUNA SCHWARMA KEBABS

The aromatic flavors that infuse the schwarma marinade add a distinct Middle Eastern tang to this dish. Serve hot off the grill or at room temperature, and feel free to substitute chicken chunks for the tuna. This recipe was adapted from one in Rise' Routenberg and Barbara Wasser's *Divine Kosher Cuisine: Catering to Family and Friends* (Divine Kosher Cuisine, 2006).

1/4 teaspoon ground black pepper
1/4 teaspoon cayenne pepper
1/4 teaspoon ground cinnamon
1/4 teaspoon salt
1/4 teaspoon ground allspice
1/4 teaspoon ground cloves
1 teaspoon ground cardamom
2 1/2 tablespoons freshly squeezed lemon juice
2 tablespoons canola oil
2 pounds tuna fillets, cut into 1-inch cubes
2 large onions, cut into 1-inch pieces
2 red bell peppers, cut into 1-inch pieces

In a shallow dish, combine the peppers, cinnamon, salt, allspice, cloves, cardamom, lemon juice, and oil. Place the tuna in the marinade and turn to coat on all sides. Cover and refrigerate for one hour.

Soak 8 12-inch wooden skewers in water for about 10 minutes to prevent them from burning while grilling. Preheat the grill or broiler 10 minutes before cooking.

Remove the tuna and marinade from the refrigerator and discard the marinade. Skewer the tuna, onions, and bell peppers, alternately. Grill the kebabs, uncovered, until the tuna has reached the desired degree of doneness.
Yield: 8 servings

GRILLED HALIBUT

Since Sheri discovered the wonders of halibut several years ago on an Alaskan adventure, this recipe, courtesy of her friend Mark Edwards, has been a big hit at her family's table. The Colemans especially enjoy this recipe's savory South American flavors and its tangy citrus bite.

5 tablespoons canola oil
2 white onions, peeled and sliced
2 shallots, peeled and sliced
2 zucchini, peeled and sliced
2 yellow squash, peeled and sliced
2 green apples, peeled and sliced
Salt
Ground black pepper
1 teaspoon ground cumin
1 teaspoon ground coriander
2 teaspoons saffron threads
1 cup freshly squeezed orange juice
1/3 cup freshly squeezed lemon juice
4 (8-ounce) halibut fillets, skin removed
16 spears asparagus, washed and trimmed

In a large pot, add 4 tablespoons of the oil and heat slightly over medium heat. Add the onion, shallot, zucchini, squash, and apples, using a wooden spoon to stir and combine. Season to taste with salt and pepper. Add 1 cup water. Bring to a boil and lower the heat to medium. Cook, covered, for 10 to 15 minutes, until the vegetables are tender. Stir in the cumin, coriander, and saffron along with the orange and lemon juices. Continue cooking, uncovered, for an additional 10 minutes. Puree the mixture in batches in a blender until smooth. Adjust the seasonings as needed. Pass through a fine mesh strainer.

Coat the fish with the remaining oil. Sprinkle with salt and pepper. Preheat a grill pan large enough to hold the fillets.

While the grill is heating, steam the asparagus until tender.

When the grill is ready, cook the fish for 3 to 4 minutes on each side, or until desired doneness, turning once.

Spoon 1/2 cup of the strained emulsion onto 4 dinner plates. Arrange the asparagus spears on the top of the sauce. Place a piece of the fish on top of the asparagus.

Yield: 4 servings

SALMON and BLUEBERRY SALAD with RED ONION VINAIGRETTE

This lovely, colorful dish for entertaining is courtesy of the U.S. Highbush Blueberry Council.

1 medium red onion, thinly sliced in half rings
1/4 cup red wine vinegar
1 teaspoon sugar
1 teaspoon salt, divided
1/4 teaspoon freshly ground black pepper, divided
3 tablespoons canola oil
1 1/2 pounds salmon fillet, cut crosswise in 4 pieces
6 cups lettuce leaves, torn into bite-sized pieces
1 cup fresh blueberries

In a microwave-safe dish, combine the onion, vinegar, sugar, 1/2 teaspoon of the salt, and 1/8 teaspoon of the pepper. Cover loosely with plastic wrap and microwave on high for 1 minute. Remove from the oven and let stand, stirring occasionally, until the onions turn pink, about 15 minutes.

Meanwhile, preheat the grill or broiler. Brush 1 tablespoon of the oil on both sides of the salmon fillets and sprinkle with the remaining salt and pepper. Grill or broil the salmon, skin side down, until it is just cooked through, about 6 minutes.

Divide the lettuce leaves among four dinner plates. Place salmon in the center of each plate of greens. With a slotted spoon, remove the onions from the vinegar. Scatter the onions, along with the blueberries, over and around the fish. Whisk the remaining oil into the vinegar mixture and drizzle the vinaigrette over the salmon.

Yield: 4 servings

HERBED PAN-FRIED FISH

This recipe was adapted from one in Sherron Goldstein's *Fresh Fields: Entertaining with Southern Comfort.*

3 tablespoons sea salt
1/4 cup sugar
3 teaspoons Tabasco
2 heads of garlic, peeled and crushed
1 tablespoon Greek seasoning
1 quart plus 1 cup regular or low-fat buttermilk
2 1/2 to 3 pounds grouper or halibut
2 cups flour
2 teaspoons freshly ground black pepper
1/2 cup Italian seasoning
1 large egg
1 teaspoon baking powder
1/2 teaspoon baking soda
Canola oil for frying
1/2 cup fresh chopped herbs, for garnish, optional

In a large plastic freezer bag, combine the sea salt, sugar, pepper sauce, garlic, and Greek seasoning. Add 1 quart of the buttermilk to the bag and mix well. Add the fish, seal the bag, and turn it to coat the fish. Refrigerate for 1 to 2 hours.

Remove the fish from the marinade and place it on a wire rack to drain. Combine the flour, pepper, and Italian seasoning together in large bag or in a pie pan. Beat together the egg, baking powder, and baking soda, and the remaining buttermilk. Dip the fish in the flour mixture and shake well to remove any excess flour. Then dip it in the buttermilk-egg mixture and coat well. Drain and dip in flour again. Remove the excess flour and place the fish on a wire rack to drain.

In a 12-inch cast-iron skillet, heat enough oil to cover the bottom of the pan on medium-high heat. Turn the heat down to medium and pan-fry the fish for about 5 minutes on each side, until the crust is golden brown. Fish fillets that are more than 1 inch thick may require a longer cooking time. Do not crowd the fish in the pan and be careful when turning the fish. Remove the fish from the pan and drain on a wire rack. Garnish with additional herbs.

Yield: 6 servings

SALMON BAKE with PECAN-CRUNCH TOPPING

Canola oil spray for greasing
4 (4- to 6-ounce) salmon fillets
1/8 teaspoon salt
1/8 teaspoon freshly ground black pepper
1 1/2 tablespoons honey
2 tablespoons Dijon mustard
2 tablespoons canola oil
1/4 cup soft breadcrumbs
1/4 cup finely chopped pecans
2 teaspoons chopped fresh parsley

Preheat the oven to 450°F. Grease a 13x9-inch ovenproof pan with the spray. Sprinkle the salmon with the salt and pepper and place in the prepared pan. In a small bowl, combine the honey, mustard, and oil and brush on top of the fish. In another bowl, combine the breadcrumbs, pecans, and parsley and spoon on top of each fillet. Bake until the fillets flake easily when tested with a fork, about 10 to 15 minutes.

This dish can also be made with a whole fillet, rather than in individual serving sizes.

Yield: 4 servings

SALMON FILLET with
SQUASH and KUMQUATS

Kumquats make a delicious sweet-tart accompaniment to salmon. These tasty foil-wrapped packets bake just long enough to perfectly steam the fish and crookneck squash. If you prefer, you may substitute halibut, red snapper, cod, or chicken tenders for the salmon. This recipe was adapted from one in Cathy Thomas and Nick Koon's *Melissa's Great Book of Produce: Everything You Need to Know about Fresh Fruits and Vegetables*.

1 1/2 pound center-cut salmon fillet
Salt
Freshly ground black pepper
6 kumquats
2 tablespoons extra-virgin olive oil, divided
1 large onion, chopped
1 large garlic clove, minced
2 to 3 crookneck squash, trimmed and cut into 1/2-inch slices
2 tablespoons canola oil
1 1/2 tablespoons sliced fresh chives or scallions
Fresh Italian parsley, chopped, for garnish

Move the oven rack to the middle position. Preheat the oven to 425°F. Remove the pin bones and skin from the salmon fillet. Cut the fillet crosswise into 4 equal pieces. Each salmon piece will probably be thinner at one end. Fold the thin portion of the fish under to create a similar thickness all the way across. Season with salt and pepper to taste. Tear 4 squares of aluminum foil, about 18x18 inches. Place 1 piece of salmon in the center of each.

Cut 2 of the kumquats into 1/8-inch slices and remove the large seeds from each slice. Set aside. Chop the remaining 4 kumquats into a fine dice.

In a medium, heavy-bottomed skillet, heat 1 tablespoon of olive oil over medium-high heat. Add the onion and cook, stirring frequently, until nicely browned. Add the garlic, half of the kumquat slices, and the squash. Cook 2 to 3 minutes, stirring frequently. Season with salt and pepper to taste. Spoon the mixture over the salmon, dividing it among the 4 servings. Seal the foil packets, scrunching the sides together, and place on a jelly roll pan. Bake 10 to 12 minutes.

To prepare the relish, combine the remaining olive oil and the canola oil, the finely chopped kumquats, and the chives. Stir to blend. Season to taste with salt and pepper.

When packets have finished baking, open each and slide contents onto four dinner plates. Spoon some of the relish on top of each serving and top with parsley. Garnish with the remaining kumquat slices.

Yield: 4 servings

TROUT with ALMONDS

This recipe is easy and classic.

2 whole (10-ounce) trout, pan-dressed
Salt
Ground black pepper
1/4 cup flour
2 tablespoons canola oil, divided
2 tablespoons canola margarine, divided
1/2 cup blanched slivered almonds
2 tablespoons freshly squeezed lemon juice
1 tablespoon chopped fresh parsley
8 slices lemon, for garnish

Rinse the trout and pat it dry. Season the fish inside and out with salt and pepper to taste. Dredge the trout in flour. Heat 1 tablespoon of the oil and 1 tablespoon of the margarine in a large skillet over high heat until the margarine has melted. Add the trout to the pan and brown on both sides. Lower the heat to medium and cook for about 5 minutes on each side or until the fish is cooked through.

Remove the trout to a serving plate and keep warm. Wipe out the pan and add the remaining oil and margarine and heat over medium heat until they just begin to brown. Add the almonds and brown.

Pour the sauce and almonds over the fish and sprinkle with lemon juice and parsley. Garnish with lemon slices.

Yield: 2 servings

SHRIMP CREOLE

2 tablespoons canola margarine
1 tablespoon flour
1 cup finely chopped onion
1 cup finely chopped celery
1 (28-ounce) can tomatoes, drained, with 1 cup liquid saved
1 green pepper, seeded and diced
1/2 teaspoon dried thyme
2 tablespoons chopped fresh parsley
2 bay leaves
1/2 teaspoon garlic powder
1 tablespoon paprika
1/4 teaspoon cayenne
Salt
1 1/2 pounds shrimp, shelled and deveined
2 tablespoons cornstarch
1/4 cup water

In a large skillet over medium heat, melt the margarine. Whisk in the flour, stirring constantly. Cook for 1 or 2 minutes until golden brown, being careful not to burn.

Add the onion and celery and continue cooking and stirring for 3 minutes. Add the tomatoes and the reserved liquid to the skillet along with the green pepper, thyme, parsley, bay leaves, garlic powder, paprika, cayenne, and salt. Cover the pan, reduce the heat to simmer, and cook, stirring occasionally, for 20 minutes.

Add the shrimp to the mixture and bring to a boil. Cook for about 3 minutes or until shrimp are pink and firm. Be careful not to overcook the shrimp.

Combine the cornstarch and water in a small bowl, mixing well, and stir this mixture into the shrimp mixture. Cook over low heat for another 2 or 3 minutes. Remove the bay leaves and discard.

Serve the shrimp creole over boiled white rice.

Yield: 6 servings

CHAPTER 7

Salads

CLIFTON BEACH
SALAD DRESSING

A friend in Cleveland, Ohio, gave Sheilah this recipe over 35 years ago, when she first taught cooking in a department store there.

1 (10 1/2-ounce) can tomato soup
1 teaspoon dry mustard
1 tablespoon Worcestershire sauce
1 teaspoon paprika
1 garlic clove, minced
1 1/2 cups canola oil
1/2 cup vinegar
1/2 cup sugar
1 teaspoon salt
1/2 teaspoon freshly ground black pepper

In a large bowl, whisk together all of the ingredients. Beat with an electric mixer or pour into a glass jar with a lid and shake well. Keep refrigerated.
Yield: 1 quart

BABY GREENS with
MAPLE CITRUS DRESSING

This salad is topped with a finger-licking dressing that you can make in minutes. For a richer flavor, try using a cold-pressed canola oil.

Juice of 2 oranges
Juice of 1 lemon
2 tablespoons maple syrup (more if you like a sweeter dressing)
1/2 cup canola oil
4 oranges, sectioned, or 1 can mandarin oranges
1/2 cup pecans, toasted
1 (16-ounce) bag baby greens or spinach

Combine the orange and lemon juices with the maple syrup and canola oil. Toss the orange slices and toasted pecans with the baby greens. Drizzle with dressing.
Yield: 6 to 8 servings

CRANBERRY
VINAIGRETTE

This vinaigrette is great on mixed greens with dried cranberries, blue cheese, and walnuts.

1/2 cup cranberries
1/2 cup red wine vinegar
1/2 cup canola oil
1/2 cup honey
1/4 teaspoon cumin
Salt
Freshly ground black pepper

Combine all of the ingredients in a blender and blend until smooth.
Yield: 2 cups

CLASSIC THREE-BEAN SALAD

This recipe, courtesy of cooking teacher Paula Jacobson, is perfect for outdoor entertaining.

1 cup red wine vinegar
3/4 cup sugar
1/2 cup canola oil
2 medium garlic cloves, minced
1 tablespoon plus 1 teaspoon kosher salt, divided
Freshly ground black pepper
8 ounces green beans, cut into 1-inch pieces
8 ounces yellow wax beans, cut into 1-inch pieces
1 (16-ounce) can red kidney beans, rinsed and drained
1/2 medium red onion, chopped
1/4 cup fresh parsley, minced

Heat vinegar, sugar, oil, garlic, 1 teaspoon of the salt, and pepper to taste in small nonreactive saucepan over medium heat, stirring occasionally, until sugar dissolves, about 5 minutes. Transfer to a large nonreactive bowl and cool to room temperature.

Bring 3 quarts of water to a boil in large saucepan over high heat. Add the remaining salt and the green and yellow beans. Cook until crisp-tender, about 5 minutes.

Meanwhile, fill a medium bowl with ice water. When the beans are done, drain them and immediately plunge them into the ice water to stop the cooking process. Let the beans sit until chilled, about 2 minutes. Drain well.

Add the green and yellow beans, kidney beans, onion, and parsley to the vinegar mixture; toss well to coat. Cover and refrigerate overnight to let the flavors meld. Let stand at room temperature 30 minutes before serving. The salad can be covered and refrigerated up to 4 days.

Yield: 8 to 10 servings

COLD MARINATED VEGETABLES

This Kaufman family favorite is courtesy of Jeanette Miller, Paula Jacobson's mother. Fresh vegetables may be substituted for the canned vegetables, if you wish.

The marinade:
2 tablespoons vinegar
6 tablespoons canola oil
1 teaspoon salt
1 teaspoon dry mustard
Ground black pepper
1 clove garlic, split
1 teaspoon dried parsley
1 teaspoon dried tarragon
1 teaspoon dried chives
1 teaspoon dried chervil

The vegetables:
1 (15-ounce) can sliced carrots, drained
1 head cauliflower, broken into florets
1 (15-ounce) can sliced beets (not pickled), drained
1 (15-ounce) can asparagus, drained
1 (15-ounce) can wax beans, drained
1 (15-ounce) can green beans, drained
1 hard-boiled egg pressed through a strainer or ricer

In a large bowl, combine all of the marinade ingredients. Cover and refrigerate for 3 to 5 hours.

Arrange the vegetables on a serving platter, sprinkle egg over the vegetables, and pour marinade over all. Cover and refrigerate until serving.

Yield: 12 servings

HONEYDEW WALNUT SALAD

If you've accidentally opened an underripe honeydew, don't fret! You can use the underripe fruit in this recipe. The honeydew's firm texture makes this salad special. This recipe is courtesy of Janet Ballantyne, Sheilah's fresh fruit and vegetable maven and the author of the *Joy of Gardening Cookbook*.

4 cups slightly underripe honeydew, cubed
1 cup walnuts, roasted
4 tablespoons minced fresh parsley
1 cup diced celery
1 cup finely diced bell red pepper
4 tablespoons freshly squeezed lime juice
2 teaspoons honey
2 tablespoons white vinegar
1/2 cup canola oil
1 teaspoon salt
Freshly ground black pepper

In a large salad bowl, toss the melon, walnuts, parsley, celery, and bell pepper.

In a small bowl or liquid measuring cup, whisk together the remaining ingredients and pour over the salad. Toss to coat. Serve at once or chill if desired.

Yield: 6 servings

JICAMA and PAPAYA SALAD

This recipe has been adapted from one in Cathy Thomas and Nick Koon's *Melissa's Great Book of Produce: Everything You Need to Know about Fresh Fruits and Vegetables* (Wiley, 2006). This colorful salad is a delectable accompaniment to grilled poultry, fish, or meat, and it can be prepared two hours in advance and refrigerated in an airtight container.

3 tablespoons freshly squeezed orange juice
1/4 teaspoon orange zest
1 1/2 teaspoons sugar, optional
1/2 teaspoon salt, plus additional to taste
2 tablespoons cider vinegar
3 tablespoons canola oil
12 ounces jicama, peeled and cut into sticks about 1 1/2 inches
    long x 3/8 inches wide (about 2 cups)
1 large (1 to 1 1/2-pound) ripe papaya, or 1 to 1 1/2 pounds
    mango
1/4 cup chopped cilantro
2 heads Bibb lettuce, washed and drained
Orange slices or orange wedges for garnish

In small bowl, whisk the juice, zest, sugar (if using), salt, and vinegar. Add the oil in a steady stream, whisking constantly. Set aside.

Place the jicama in medium-large bowl. Peel the papaya and cut it in half. Scoop out and discard the seeds. Cut lengthwise into 1 1/4-inch strips. Cut the strips into 1/2-inch crosswise slices and add to the jicama. Add the dressing and cilantro and gently toss. Arrange the lettuce on a platter. Top with the jicama mixture. If desired, garnish with orange slices or wedges.

Yield: 6 servings

LENTIL and
SPINACH SALAD

We attended a mouthwatering prairie picnic hosted by Chef Penny Barr of Unique Chic when we were in Moose Jaw, Saskatchewan. This is one of her superb recipes.

1/3 cup balsamic vinegar
1/3 cup red wine vinegar
1/4 cup canola oil
Handful of dried cherries or cranberries
5 cups fresh spinach, washed and patted dry
1 cup cooked green lentils (preferably French)
Salt
Ground black pepper
Juice of 1 lime or lemon
1/2 of a red onion, sliced, optional
1/2 cup feta cheese, optional

In a small bowl, whisk together the vinegars and oil. Set aside.

In a large bowl, place the cherries or cranberries (or a mixture of both), the spinach, and the lentils. Season with salt and pepper to taste, and pour the lime juice over the top. Serve with the dressing on the side, or pour it over the salad and mix well. Before serving, add the sliced red onions, feta, and any other vegetables or toppings you'd like.

Yield: 6 to 8 servings

Hint: Spinach will keep longer if it is stored loose in the vegetable drawer of your refrigerator rather than if it is kept in a plastic bag. The leaves can't breathe well in plastic bags and this causes the cells to die and rot.

MIMOSA CAULIFLOWER SALAD

This recipe, courtesy of Sheilah's friend Polly Clingerman, makes a beautiful centerpiece for a holiday buffet.

1 large cauliflower
2 teaspoons freshly squeezed lemon juice
1 teaspoon salt
2 tablespoons fresh chives or parsley, chopped
1/2 cup scallions, chopped
8 hard-cooked eggs, finely chopped
4 teaspoons Dijon mustard
2 teaspoons seasoned salt
1 1/2 cups canola oil
1/2 cup white wine vinegar
Lettuce leaves, washed and dried

Leave the cauliflower head whole, but remove all of the green leaves. In a large pot, bring 2 cups of water to a boil, add the lemon juice, salt, and cauliflower. Simmer, uncovered, for 10 to 20 minutes, until the cauliflower is crisp-tender. Remove the cauliflower from the pot, drain, and cool to lukewarm.

In a medium bowl whisk together the chives, scallions, chopped eggs, mustard, seasoned salt, oil, and vinegar.

Line a serving platter with lettuce leaves. Place the cauliflower on top. Pour half of the sauce over it, taking care to coat the cauliflower completely and uniformly. Refrigerate for at least 2 hours so the flavors can penetrate.

Serve chilled or at room temperature. Serve the remaining sauce separately.

Yield: 6 servings

ORANGES in HONEY

This recipe has been adapted from one in Penelope Casas' *Paella! Spectacular Rice Dishes from Spain* (Henry Holt, 1999). This salad is not only beautiful to look at but will have you coming back for seconds or more!

6 naval oranges
2 tablespoons honey
1 1/2 cups sugar
2 tablespoons canola oil
2 tablespoons orange liqueur
Fresh mint leaves, cut into julienne, for garnish

Remove thin strips of peel from 2 oranges and cut into a very fine julienne. Juice one of the peeled oranges, reserving the juice, and finish peeling the other. Peel the remaining 4 oranges being careful to remove the pith (the bitter white covering the orange) from each one.

Place the julienned peel in a small pan with only enough water to cover it. Bring the water to a boil, reduce the heat to simmer, and cook for 10 minutes. Drain well and run under cold water. Set aside.

In a 2-quart saucepan, bring to a boil the honey, sugar, reserved orange juice, and 1/2 cup water. Boil slowly until the liquid is syrupy and reads 230°F on a candy thermometer, about 10 minutes. Add the julienned orange peel and remove the pan from the heat.

When the liquid is cool, stir in the oil and liqueur. Slice the oranges and arrange them in overlapping concentric circles in a large shallow bowl or serving platter. Pour the cooled syrup over the oranges and let the salad sit at room temperature for 1 hour or longer. Just before serving, garnish with mint if desired.

Yield: 3/4 to 1 cup

Hint: If you scratch the peel of a piece of citrus fruit with your nail, the aroma will indicate the sweetness of the fruit.

PICNIC BEAN SALAD

This delightful, colorful, and healthy salad had been adapted from one on the Peak of the Market website (www.PeakMarket.com).

The salad:
1 pound yellow beans
1 pound green beans
1 (19-ounce) can red kidney beans, drained
1 (19-ounce) can lima beans, drained
1 (19-ounce) can chickpeas, drained
1 (19-ounce) can pinto beans, drained
2 green bell peppers, chopped
2 Bermuda onions, thinly sliced

The marinade:
1/2 cup red wine vinegar
1/4 cup canola oil
1/3 cup sugar
1/3 cup brown sugar, packed
Freshly ground black pepper
Salt

Snap the ends off of the yellow and green beans and cut into 1 1/2-inch pieces. Cook the beans in boiling water for 3 minutes. Plunge them into cold water until cool, then drain them, and pat them dry.

In a large bowl, combine the cooked beans, kidney beans, lima beans, chickpeas, pinto beans, pepper, and onions.

In a medium bowl, combine the vinegar, oil, sugars, and pepper and salt to taste. Stir into the bean mixture. Cover and marinate in the refrigerator overnight.

Yield: 20 servings

NORTH DAKOTA GERMAN POTATO SALAD

People of many nationalities call North Dakota their home, and the Germans are among the strongest of these groups. Before moving to North Dakota in the late 1970s, I had known only the standard creamy version of potato salad, but this German variation is a real treat. This recipe has excellent flavor and will be a hit at your next picnic. It contains no mayonnaise and can be served warm or cold.

2 pounds potatoes
1 pound bacon
1/3 cup plus 3 tablespoons canola oil, divided
1 onion, chopped
3 tablespoons brown mustard
6 tablespoons white wine vinegar
1/4 cup thinly sliced scallions
2 tablespoons fresh parsley

Peel the potatoes, cut them into 2-inch cubes, and place them in a large pot. Add enough water to the pot to just cover the potatoes. Bring to boil and then simmer over medium-low heat for 20 minutes or until the potatoes can be easily pierced by a fork but will not fall apart.

Fry the bacon until crisp according to package directions, and dry on paper towels. When cool, crumble.

In a skillet over medium heat, heat 3 tablespoons of the oil. Add the onions and sauté until clear and golden.

Combine the bacon, the onion, the remaining oil, the mustard, and the vinegar in a large bowl. Add the potatoes and scallions. Toss together. Sprinkle with the parsley and salt and pepper to taste.

Yield: 8 servings

RED, WHITE, and BLUE
POTATO SALAD

An assortment of baby potatoes (called creamers) cooked in their skins creates a colorful dish. This salad uses a patriotic mix of red, white, and blue spuds, but if you prefer, you can substitute fingerling varieties and adjust the cooking time as needed. For a flakier version, use russet or Yukon gold potatoes. Peel them when they are cool enough to handle and cut them into bite-size chunks before tossing with dressing. This recipe has been adapted from one in Cathy Thomas and Nick Koon's *Melissa's Great Book of Produce: Everything You Need to Know about Fresh Fruits and Vegetables* (Wiley, 2006).

4 sprigs fresh thyme
1 sprig fresh rosemary
1 cup dry white wine
2 medium cloves garlic
1/2 pound red creamers, cleaned
1/2 pound purple creamers, cleaned
1/2 pound white creamers, cleaned
1 tablespoon plus 2 teaspoons kosher salt, divided
1/4 cup white wine vinegar
1 tablespoon whole-grain mustard
 Freshly ground black pepper
1/2 cup canola oil
2 stalks celery, trimmed and thinly sliced
2 tablespoons minced fresh Italian parsley
2 scallions (including dark green stalks), thinly sliced

Place the thyme, rosemary, white wine, and garlic in large saucepan or Dutch oven. Cut the potatoes into 1-inch cubes, leaving the skin intact. Place in the pan and add cold water to cover by 1 inch. Add 1 tablespoon of the salt. Bring to a boil on high heat. Reduce the heat to medium and boil gently until the potatoes are tender, about 10 to 12 minutes.

Meanwhile, prepare the dressing. In a large bowl, combine the vinegar, the mustard, the remaining salt, and pepper to taste. Whisk in the oil in a thin stream.

Drain the potatoes and discard the herbs. Gently toss the warm potatoes with enough dressing to coat. Add the celery and toss again. Let cool.

Add the parsley and scallions and gently toss. Taste and adjust seasoning if needed. Serve at room temperature.

Yield: 6 servings

SPICED SALAD CROUTONS

These homemade croutons will taste better than anything you can find in the store. The spice measurements are just guidance: go ahead and experiment with amounts.

1/4 cup cayenne pepper
1/2 teaspoon dried basil
1/2 teaspoon dried oregano
1/2 teaspoon salt
1/2 teaspoon freshly ground black pepper
1/2 teaspoon garlic powder
1/3 cup canola oil
4 cups French bread, cubed

In a medium bowl combine the cayenne, basil, oregano, salt, pepper, and garlic powder. Set aside.

Heat the canola oil in a large nonstick skillet over medium-high heat. When the oil is warm, add the bread, toss to coat in the oil, and sauté until toasted to a golden brown, about 5 minutes. Remove the bread from the skillet and add to the bowl with the seasonings. Toss to coat. After the croutons have cooled, place them in a resealable plastic bag for up to one week.

Yield: 4 cups

SPINACH SALAD with
CITRUS VINAIGRETTE

The salad:

1 (16-ounce) package fresh spinach, stems removed

1/2 red onion, thinly sliced

1 1/2 cups mushrooms, sliced

1/4 cup crumbled crisp bacon or vegetarian bacon substitute

The dressing:

1/2 cup freshly squeezed orange juice

1/4 cup canola oil

1 garlic clove, minced

2 tablespoons sugar

1 tablespoon white vinegar

Freshly ground black pepper

Place the spinach in a large salad bowl and mix in the onion, mushrooms, and bacon.

To prepare the dressing, combine the orange juice, oil, garlic, sugar, and vinegar. Pour the dressing on the salad and lightly toss. Add pepper to taste.

Yield: 4 to 6 servings

SPINACH SALAD with
GRAPES and ORANGES

Healthy as well as delicious, this combination of romaine, spinach, fruits, and nuts can't be beat. If desired, add a little more curry.

1 head romaine leaves, torn into pieces
1 cup fresh spinach, torn into pieces
1 (11-ounce) can mandarin orange sections, drained and chilled
1 cup white grapes, halved and seeded
1/2 cup slivered almonds, toasted
1/2 cup canola oil
1/3 cup white wine vinegar
1 garlic clove, minced
2 tablespoons minced fresh chives
1 tablespoon curry powder
1 teaspoon soy sauce
2 tablespoons brown sugar, packed

In a large bowl, combine the lettuce, spinach, oranges, grapes, and almonds.

In a jar with a tight-fitting lid, combine the oil, vinegar, garlic, chives, curry powder, soy sauce, and brown sugar. Shake well.

Just before serving, toss some of the dressing with the salad and serve the remaining dressing on the side.

Yield: 6 to 8 servings

TOMATO and BASIL PASTA SALAD

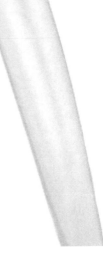

Lovely to look at, delightful to eat, this dish, adapted from a recipe in Sherron Goldstein's *Fresh Fields: Entertaining with Southern Comfort*, is perfect for entertaining. Sherron feels "food is an expression of love," and when you serve this recipe, you and your family and friends will understand what she means. This salad can be prepared an hour or two before serving.

4 large tomatoes, seeded and cut into 8 sections
1 large cucumber, seeded and chopped
1 broccoli top, blanched and cut into bite-sized pieces
1 medium red onion, thinly sliced
3 yellow squash, blanched and sliced
1 cup fresh basil, torn
1 pound penne pasta, cooked according to package directions
4 tablespoons canola oil
Store-bought red wine vinaigrette

Toss all of the ingredients with the pasta and add the vinaigrette to taste. Refrigerate 1 to 2 hours before serving.
Yield: 8 servings

Hint: Fresh tomatoes keep better longer if they are stored on your countertop with the stems down. Never store tomatoes in the refrigerator.

WILD RICE SALAD

This recipe, courtesy of cookbook author Nathalie Dupree, can be served warm or at room temperature. A great party dish, the recipe can easily be doubled.

The salad:
1 cup wild rice, rinsed thoroughly
1/2 cup dried cranberries
1/4 cup chopped dried apricots
1/4 cup finely chopped scallions
1 cup chopped walnuts or pecans, optional

The dressing:
2 tablespoons red wine vinegar
1 tablespoon freshly squeezed lemon juice
2 garlic cloves, finely chopped
1 teaspoon Dijon mustard
1 teaspoon sugar
Salt
Freshly ground black pepper
3/4 cup canola oil

In a large pan, cook the rice according to package directions.

To make the dressing, process the vinegar, lemon juice, garlic, mustard, sugar, and salt and pepper to taste in a blender until smooth. Slowly whisk in the oil. (The dressing can be made 3 to 4 days ahead and refrigerated.)

In a large bowl, combine the rice, cranberries, apricots, scallions, and nuts, if using. Pour enough dressing over the rice to coat it lightly. Save the leftover dressing. If you prepare the salad in the morning, you can refresh it with a little dressing prior to serving.

Yield: 4 to 6 servings

WATERMELON and RED ONION SALAD

Sheilah adapted this recipe from one in Hugh Carpenter and Terri Sandison's *Fusion Food Cookbook* (Artisan, 1994), the first Hugh Carpenter book she bought. The contrasting tastes and textures of the watermelon and thin crisp red onions, heightened by the fresh raspberry vinaigrette, make the perfect beginning to any dinner.

Raspberry essence:
12 ounces frozen raspberries
1 (750-milliliter) bottle red wine
1 cup sugar
1/4 teaspoon ground black pepper

The dressing:
1/4 cup raspberry vinegar
2 tablespoons finely minced shallots
1 tablespoon honey
1/4 cup canola oil
1 teaspoon Asian chili sauce

The salad:
2 medium red onions, peeled and thinly sliced
2 bunches watercress
3 pounds fresh watermelon, preferably both red and yellow
1/4 cup anise hyssop or other fresh mint leaves
Fresh berries, for garnish

In a nonreactive skillet, combine the raspberries, wine, sugar, and pepper. Place over high heat and bring to a vigorous boil. Boil until only 2 cups remain. Immediately pour the sauce through a medium meshed sieve, forcing all the pulp through the sieve by scraping the sieve with a metal spoon. Cover and refrigerate 3 to 5 hours or until chilled. This "raspberry essence" lasts indefinitely. It may need to be thinned slightly with a liqueur or water before using.

In a medium bowl, combine 6 tablespoons of the raspberry essence and the remaining dressing ingredients. (The rest of the essence may be reserve for a later use.) Taste the dressing and adjust the seasonings.

Separate the onion slices into individual rings. Toss with the salad dressing and marinate for 2 hours in the refrigerator, turning every 30 minutes.

Remove and discard the woody stems from the watercress, and then refrigerate the sprigs.

Cut enough watermelon into 1- to 2-inch cubes, rectangles, or other shapes, knocking away the seeds, to yield 8 cups. Refrigerate the watermelon.

Cut the mint leaves into shreds and set aside. The recipe can be completed up to this point 8 hours in advance of serving.

To assemble the salad, arrange a bed of watercress on 6 chilled plates and top with watermelon slices. Arrange the onions attractively on the watermelon. Drizzle the salad dressing over the melon and onions. Garnish with mint and fresh berries and serve at once.

Yield: 6 side salads

CHAPTER 8

Vegetables and Side Dishes

ASIAN-STYLE HONEY VEGETABLE STIR-FRY

1/4 cup stir-fry sauce
1/4 cup honey
Crushed red pepper
4 tablespoons canola oil
2 cups eggplant, cut into 1/2-inch cubes
2 cups red bell pepper, cut into 1/2-inch pieces
1 small onion, cut into wedges and separated
1 medium carrot, cut diagonally
Garlic powder

Combine the stir-fry sauce with the honey and crushed red pepper to taste in a small bowl.

In wok or large skillet, heat the oil over medium-high heat, add the eggplant, bell pepper, onion, carrot, and garlic powder to taste. Toss and cook for about 2 to 3 minutes. Add the honey sauce and stir until all of the vegetables are glazed and sauce is bubbly hot, about 1 minute. Serve as a side dish or over steamed rice or noodles as a main dish.
Yield: 4 to 6 servings

BAKED FENNEL PARMESAN

This side dish is a refreshing change of taste.

Canola oil spray for greasing
3 heads fennel
2 cups milk
1/2 onion, sliced
Freshly ground black pepper
Salt
2 teaspoons canola margarine
3/4 to 1 cup freshly grated Parmesan cheese
2 tablespoons dried breadcrumbs
1 tablespoon canola oil

Preheat the oven to 425°F. Grease a baking dish with the spray. Trim and remove the fennel stalks but leave the bulbs whole.

In a pan over medium heat, bring the milk, onion, and 2 quarts water to a boil. Add the fennel, reduce the heat to simmer, and cook until tender. Drain well, saving 1/4 cup of the cooking liquid. Trim, halve, and core the fennel. Place it in the prepared dish and sprinkle with salt and pepper to taste. Dot the top with the margarine and sprinkle with the cheese, breadcrumbs, and reserved cooking liquid. Place in the oven until heated through. Drizzle with oil and serve.
Yield: 6 to 8 servings

BROCCOLI and
CHEESE FRITTERS

Sheilah first tasted this recipe in a hotel in Miami in the 1970s. It is still a favorite.

2 cups flour
3 large eggs
1 cup milk
1 tablespoon baking powder
1 1/2 teaspoons salt
1/2 teaspoon Worcestershire sauce
2 drops Tabasco
2 cups broccoli florets, cooked, cooled, and drained well
1 cup grated sharp cheddar cheese
Canola oil for frying
Sweet and sour sauce, or your favorite dipping sauce

In a large bowl mix together the flour, eggs, milk, baking powder, salt, Worcestershire, and Tabasco. Gently fold in the broccoli and cheese. Heat enough oil to cover the bottom of a skillet or frying pan, and drop the batter by spoonfuls into the oil. Cook until golden brown on all sides, about 3 minutes per side, turning once. Drain well on paper towels and serve with sweet and sour sauce for dipping.

Yield: 12 fritters, or 6 side dish servings.

BAKED TOMATOES
STUFFED with COUSCOUS

These incredible stuffed tomatoes can be served hot or warm as a side dish or first course, or warm or cold at a picnic or tailgate party. Of course, the more flavorful the tomatoes, the more flavorful the dish. If your tomatoes lack sweetness, try sprinkling a tiny bit of sugar inside the hollow shells. For a quick variation, 3 cups of cooked rice may be substituted for the couscous. The couscous mixture can be prepared up to 2 days ahead and stored in an airtight container in the refrigerator. The tomatoes can be hollowed out up to 2 hours before baking. This recipe has been adapted from one in Cathy Thomas and Nick Koon's *Melissa's Great Book of Produce: Everything You Need to Know about Fresh Fruits and Vegetables*.

Canola oil spray for greasing
10 medium tomatoes
Garlic salt
Freshly ground black pepper
Pinch of sugar, optional
1 cup couscous
3/4 teaspoon salt
1/2 red onion, finely chopped
1 yellow bell pepper, cored, seeded, and finely chopped
1/2 cup golden raisins, roughly chopped
2 teaspoons Dijon mustard
1/4 cup white wine vinegar
1/4 cup olive oil
1/4 cup canola oil
1/2 cup chopped fresh basil
1/2 cup chopped fresh parsley
1/2 cup pine nuts, toasted, optional
Sprigs of watercress, for garnish

Preheat the oven to 375°F. Line a roasting pan with parchment paper or grease it lightly with the spray.

Cut the tops off of the tomatoes and set them aside. Scoop out and discard the seeds and core. Season the hollow tomatoes with garlic salt, pepper, and a pinch of sugar, if desired. Place the tomatoes, cut side down, on paper towels for at least 10 minutes.

Bring 1 1/2 cups water to a boil. In a large bowl, combine the couscous and the boiling water. Cover and let rest for about 5 minutes or until the water is absorbed. Add the salt, onion, bell pepper, and raisins and stir to combine.

In a small bowl, whisk the mustard and vinegar. Add the oils in a thin stream, whisking constantly. Season to taste with garlic salt and pepper. Stir in the basil and parsley. Add pine nuts, if using, and stir. Stir the vinaigrette into the couscous. Fill the tomatoes with couscous, place tomato tops on top of each tomato, and bake for 25 minutes. Line a platter with watercress and arrange the tomatoes on top.
Yield: 10 servings

FENNEL PLAIN
and SIMPLE

This is a simple way to prepare this fabulous vegetable.

1 tablespoon canola oil
1 tablespoon canola margarine
7 to 8 fennel stalks, coarsely chopped
1 cup water or chicken or vegetable broth
Salt
Freshly ground white or black pepper

In a large skillet over medium heat, heat the oil and margarine. Add the fennel and stir for 2 minutes, coating the vegetable with the oil and margarine. Add the water to the pan and bring to a boil. Continue to cook at a rapid boil for 4 to 5 minutes, until the liquid begins to reduce and thicken, making a sauce. Make sure to watch the pan during this stage; if too much liquid evaporates, add a little more water. Season with salt and pepper to taste. Serve warm.
Yield: 2 servings

BEST BAKED POTATOES

This recipe is courtesy of Sheri's good friend Dave Gehrtz, a great home chef with an incredible repertoire. Sheri's friend Paula says it best about this recipe: "It's so good, I could have eaten it all!"

8 to 16 ounces canola margarine, melted
1/3 cup prepared white horseradish
1/4 cup chopped garlic
20 medium potatoes, peeled and cut in half
Salt

Preheat the oven to 350°F.

In a large bowl, mix together the melted margarine, horseradish, and garlic. Dump the potatoes into the melted margarine and gently toss to cover on all sides. Place the potatoes in a shallow baking pan with the cut side up. Sprinkle with salt and bake, uncovered, until a knife slides easily into the potato, 35 to 40 minutes.

Yield: 8 to 10 servings

MARCIA MACOMB'S STIR-FRIED ASPARAGUS

For the best results, select very thin asparagus for this recipe.

1 pound asparagus
1/4 cup canola oil
1 garlic clove, minced
1 thin slice fresh ginger, minced
2 to 3 tablespoons chicken broth
2 teaspoons soy sauce

Prepare the asparagus by breaking off the bottom 2 to 3 inches of each stalk. Cut the stalks on a sharp diagonal into 1-inch pieces.

In a wok or skillet, heat the oil and quickly stir-fry the garlic and ginger. Add the asparagus and stir-fry for about 1 minute. Add 2 tablespoons of the broth, cover, and cook over medium-high heat for 4 to 5 minutes. Add more broth if needed. Just before serving, stir in the soy sauce.

Yield: 6 servings

BRUSSELS SPROUTS
with PANCETTA

Sheri's kids wouldn't eat Brussels sprouts until she started making this recipe. You'll really enjoy the sweetness of the Brussels, the smokiness of the pancetta, and the surprising zest of the citrus as they meld together in your mouth.

1 pound fresh Brussels sprouts
3 tablespoons canola oil
3 ounces pancetta or bacon, sliced thin and chopped
1 garlic clove, minced
Salt
Freshly ground black pepper
1/2 lemon

Fill a large pot half full with water and bring to a rolling boil over high heat. Carefully add the Brussels sprouts and cook for 4 minutes. Drain. When the sprouts have cooled, cut them in half.

In a large heavy skillet over medium heat, heat the oil. Add the pancetta and sauté until it begins to crisp, about 3 minutes. Add the garlic and sauté until pale golden brown, about another 2 minutes. Add the Brussels sprouts to the skillet and sauté until they are heated through and beginning to brown. Season with salt and pepper to taste. Squeeze the lemon half over the Brussels sprouts and remove the skillet from heat. Serve immediately.

Yield: 6 servings

CAJUN FRIES

These are the perfect accompaniment to grilled chicken and burgers or even fish tacos. Quick and easy, they can be made ahead of time and reheated in the oven.

2 pounds russet potatoes, cut into finger-length fries
1 cup corn flour
2 tablespoons cornmeal
2 tablespoons Cajun seasoning
1 quart canola oil for deep frying
Sea salt

Place the cut potatoes in a large bowl of cold water. Soak for 10 minutes.

In a large resealable plastic bag, combine the corn flour, cornmeal, and Cajun seasoning. Shake the bag to blend.

Drain the potatoes, but leave them wet. Place them in the plastic bag with the seasoning and shake to coat.

Heat the oil in a deep-fryer to 375°F. Cook the fries in hot oil for 7 minutes or until golden brown. Remove from the fryer to paper towels to drain. Season with sea salt to taste.

Yield: 4 to 6 servings

CARAMELIZED POTATO KUGEL

Canola oil spray for greasing
1 1/2 pounds sweet potatoes
1 1/2 pounds Yukon gold potatoes, peeled
3 tablespoons canola oil
4 medium onions, chopped
1 teaspoon chopped fresh thyme
1 tablespoon sugar
4 large eggs, beaten

Preheat the oven to 375°F. Lightly spray a 13x9-inch baking pan.

Using two separate pots, boil each type of potatoes in salted water to cover for approximately 20 minutes. Drain well, cool, and cut into slices. Arrange the potatoes in the prepared pan.

In a large skillet, heat the oil and sauté the onions and thyme until golden. Stir in the sugar and continue to cook another two minutes. Remove from heat and cool slightly.

In a medium bowl, mix the eggs and onion mixture. Pour the mixture over the potatoes and bake for 40 minutes.

Yield: 8 servings

CELERY and
MUSHROOM BAKE

This recipe is a great side dish for chicken, pork, and beef. Consider using a variety of mushrooms, and for the celery, celery hearts taste best.

4 cups sliced celery
5 tablespoons canola margarine
1 (8-ounce) can sliced water chestnuts, drained
4 ounces mushrooms, sliced
1/4 cup slivered almonds
3 tablespoons flour
1 cup chicken broth
Salt
Freshly ground black pepper
1/2 cup half-and-half
1/2 cup dry breadcrumbs
1/2 cup grated Parmesan cheese

Preheat the oven to 350°F.

In a medium saucepan bring enough water to just cover the celery to a boil. Cook the celery in the boiling water for 7 minutes or until crisp tender; drain.

Add the margarine to a large skillet over medium heat. Sauté the water chestnuts, mushrooms, and almonds in the margarine for 5 minutes, until light golden brown. Stir the flour into the chicken broth and add to the sautéed mixture. Cook until thickened, stirring constantly. Add salt and pepper to taste. Stir in the celery and half-and-half.

Pour the vegetable mixture into a greased 1 1/2-quart casserole dish. Sprinkle the breadcrumbs and cheese over the top. Bake for 30 minutes.

Yield: 4 to 6 servings

CHINESE OVEN RICE

When dinner guests call Sheilah, they say, "I know we're having oven rice, but what else are you preparing?" She has been making this dish for thirty-six years; it also appears in her cookbook, *Simply Irresistible: Easy, Elegant, Fearless, Fussless Cooking.*

2 cups long-grain white rice
1/4 cup canola oil
3 tablespoons soy sauce
1 (1-ounce) package dry onion soup mix
1 (8-ounce) can sliced mushrooms

Preheat the oven to 350°F.

In a 3-quart covered casserole dish, combine the rice, oil, soy sauce, and onion soup mix. Drain the liquid from the can of mushrooms into a liquid measuring cup and add enough water to make 4 cups of liquid. Add the mushrooms and liquid to the casserole and stir well. Cover and bake for 1 hour.

Yield: 8 servings

RICE TABBOULEH

The USA Rice Federation website offers rice recipes from around the world (www.usarice.com). This recipe by Julie DeMatteo won the 2001 Rice to the Rescue recipe contest sponsored by the federation.

3 cups cooked white rice
1 cup chopped fresh Italian flat-leaf parsley
3/4 cup chopped cucumber
3/4 cup chopped tomato
1/4 cup minced fresh mint leaves
1/4 cup canola oil
1/4 cup freshly squeezed lemon juice
1 teaspoon salt
1 teaspoon freshly ground black pepper

In a large bowl, combine all of the ingredients. Toss well.

Yield: 6 servings

CREAMED WHIPPED POTATOES

This hearty Coleman family standard is a staple at many of their holiday gatherings.

Canola oil spray for greasing
5 pounds potatoes, peeled, cubed, boiled, and mashed
1 (8-ounce) package cream cheese, softened
1 (16-ounce) carton sour cream
1/2 cup canola margarine
1/4 teaspoon garlic powder
1/4 teaspoon onion powder
Salt
Freshly ground black pepper

Preheat the oven to 350°F and grease a medium baking dish with the spray.

Whip the potatoes, cream cheese, sour cream, margarine, garlic powder, onion powder, and salt and pepper to taste with an electric mixer until smooth. Pour the whipped potatoes into the prepared dish. Bake uncovered for 30 minutes, until lightly golden brown.

Yield: 10 to 12 servings

CURRIED SWEET POTATOES

This sweet and spicy dish is an Indian version of sweet potatoes. It is easy to throw together and can be prepared ahead of time and baked the next day.

6 medium sweet potatoes
3/4 cup coconut milk
2 1/2 teaspoons Thai red curry paste
1/4 cup plus 3 tablespoons pure maple syrup, divided
4 tablespoons canola margarine, divided
1 teaspoon salt
Canola oil spray
6 teaspoons brown sugar

Preheat the oven to 350°F. Prick the sweet potatoes all over with a fork. Bake on a baking sheet until soft, about 1 hour. Let cool slightly. Peel the potatoes, transfer them to a bowl, and mash with a potato masher.

In a large saucepan over medium heat, bring the coconut milk and curry paste to a simmer. Cook for 5 minutes. Add the potatoes along with 3 tablespoons of the maple syrup, 2 tablespoons of the canola margarine, and the salt, and stir.

Preheat the oven to broil. Grease a 9x9-inch baking pan with the spray. Spoon the potato mixture into the pan and smooth the top. Drizzle with the remaining maple syrup. Dot with the remaining margarine and sprinkle with the brown sugar. Broil until the top is sizzling and browned, 3 to 4 minutes.

Yield: 6 servings

FRESH ASPARAGUS with
WILD MUSHROOMS and ROASTED PEPPERS

Asparagus is great with anything, but Sheilah especially loves it with salmon. This recipe has been adapted from one in her cookbook *Simply Irresistible: Easy, Elegant, Fearless, Fussless Cooking.*

1 tablespoon canola oil
2 teaspoons chopped garlic
1/2 pound fresh asparagus (6 to 8 stalks), trimmed and cut into 1-
    inch pieces
2 to 3 fresh shiitake mushroom caps or oyster mushrooms,
    sliced
2 tablespoons julienned roasted red peppers
Salt
Freshly ground black pepper

In a large sauté pan, heat the oil over medium-high heat for 3 to 4 minutes. Add the garlic and stir to coat with the oil. Add the asparagus and cook for 2 to 3 minutes. Add the mushrooms and cook for another 2 minutes. Lower the heat and add the roasted red peppers. Season with salt and pepper to taste.
Yield: 2 servings

GORGONZOLA
LEMON RICE

This recipe, adapted from one on the USA Rice Federation website (www.usarice.com), was created by Kelly Mapes and won the federation's Rice to the Rescue recipe contest in 2003. Another blue cheese may be substituted for the Gorgonzola.

2 tablespoons canola oil
2 cups coarsely chopped fresh mushrooms
1 (4-ounce) package Gorgonzola cheese, crumbled
1/2 cup heavy cream
2 tablespoons freshly squeezed lemon juice
1/2 teaspoon salt
1/4 teaspoon freshly ground black pepper
3 cups cooked rice
2 cups torn fresh spinach leaves, lightly packed
2 teaspoons lemon zest

Heat the oil in a large saucepan over medium heat. Add the mushrooms and cook until soft, about 4 minutes. Reduce the heat to medium-low, stir in the cheese, and continue to stir frequently until the cheese melts, for about 3 minutes. Stir in the cream, lemon juice, salt, and pepper. Stir in the rice and heat until hot, about 5 minutes. Toss in the spinach just before serving. Garnish with lemon zest.

Yield: 6 servings

HERBED GREEN BEANS

This quick and tasty way to prepare green beans is adapted from the Peak of the Market website (www.PeakMarket.com).

1 pound green beans, trimmed
1 teaspoon canola oil
1 teaspoon canola margarine
1 small onion, thinly sliced
1 garlic clove, minced
1 tablespoon chopped, fresh oregano
Salt
Freshly ground black pepper

In a large pot, bring enough water to cover the beans to a rapid boil. Cook the beans in the boiling water for 4 to 5 minutes, or until they are crisp-tender; drain.

In a heavy skillet combine the oil and margarine. Add the onion and garlic. Cook over medium-low heat, stirring occasionally, until the onion is tender. Stir in the beans, oregano, and salt and pepper to taste. Cook until heated.

Yield: 4 servings

HERBED MUSHROOMS
with WINE SAUCE

Using a variety of mushrooms gives this recipes lots of flavor. If you'd prefer mushrooms with more "meat," use portabellas. This recipe can be used as a topping for steak or a side dish.

1 tablespoon canola oil
1 1/2 pounds fresh mushrooms
1 teaspoon Italian seasoning
1/4 cup dry white wine
2 cloves garlic, minced
Salt
Freshly ground black pepper

Heat the oil in a large skillet over medium heat. Add the mushrooms and Italian seasoning to the skillet and cook 10 minutes, stirring frequently. Mix in the wine and garlic and continue cooking until most of the wine has evaporated. Season with salt and pepper to taste. *Yield: 2 cups*

SWEET POTATO FRITES

These baked frites are a quick and easy accompaniment to any meal. You can jazz them up by adding 1/4 teaspoon cayenne pepper and/or 1/2 teaspoon ground cumin before baking.

3 large sweet potatoes
2 tablespoons canola oil
1 teaspoon salt
1/2 teaspoon freshly ground black pepper

Preheat the oven to 400°F. Peel the potatoes and cut each one in half. Cut each half into 6 wedges. Place the wedges in a large mixing bowl. Add the oil, salt, and pepper. Toss until the potatoes are evenly coated.

Spread the frites in a single layer on a baking sheet. Place on the middle rack of oven. Bake the potatoes until they are cooked through and golden crisp on the edges, about 35 minutes. Serve immediately. *Yield: 6 servings*

MOM'S CROCK-POT STUFFING

You can make this recipe ahead of time and just throw it in your Crock-Pot. What could be easier? Raisin lovers may want to add 1 cup of raisins for extra flavor.

1 cup canola margarine
1 cup chopped red onion
2 cups chopped celery
2 (8-ounce) jars sliced mushrooms
1 teaspoon poultry seasoning
1 1/2 teaspoon salt
1 1/2 teaspoon dried sage
1 teaspoon dried thyme
1/2 teaspoon ground black pepper
12 cups dry breadcrumbs
2 eggs, well beaten
3 1/2 to 4 1/2 cups chicken broth

Mix the margarine, onion, and celery in a large sauté pan and sauté over medium heat until the onion is transparent. Add the mushrooms, seasonings, breadcrumbs, eggs, and broth.

Pour the mixture into a Crock-Pot. Cook on high for 45 minutes and then turn to low for 4 to 8 hours.

Yield: 10 to 12 servings

MUSHROOMS with
WHITE WINE and SOUR CREAM

This recipe is best when served on a thin toast.

2 tablespoons canola margarine
2 tablespoons canola oil
1 pound fresh mushrooms
2 tablespoons finely chopped shallots or scallions
Salt
1 teaspoon paprika
1 tablespoon flour
1/4 cup white wine
1 cup sour cream

Heat the margarine and oil in a sauté pan over medium heat. Add the mushrooms and shallots, stirring until the shallots are soft. Stir in salt to taste and the paprika, mixing well. Sprinkle the flour over the mixture evenly, mix well, and cook another minute. Add the wine and continue cooking and stirring. Stir in the sour cream. Bring the mixture just to the boiling point but do not let it boil. Serve on toast or English muffins. *Yield: 2 to 4 servings*

Hint: To prepare fresh mushrooms, first wipe them off with a dampened paper towel. Do not place them under running water or soak them, as mushrooms will absorb moisture and become soggy during cooking. Cut the tips off of the stems and proceed with your recipe.

PAN-FRIED ZUCCHINI
with TAHINI DRESSING

Dressing pan-fried vegetables with tahini is both sumptuous and healthy. Look for firm, bright green zucchini without bruises for the best results. Eggplant, peppers, and cauliflower can be sliced and substituted for or served in addition to the zucchini in this recipe. Try serving this dish as an accompaniment to grilled or roasted meats. This recipe is courtesy of Amy Riolo.

3 small zucchini
1/8 cup canola oil
1/4 cup tahini
Juice of 1 lemon
1 teaspoon olive oil
Salt
Freshly ground black pepper

Slice the zucchini in half lengthwise. Then slice them in half lengthwise again.

Slice each stick in half widthwise to make thin sticks.

In a large shallow skillet over medium heat, heat the canola oil. When the oil is hot, add the zucchini sticks. Fry for 3 to 5 minutes on each side, until they are golden brown. Remove the zucchini from the oil, place on a platter lined with paper towels, and let drain.

In a blender or mixing bowl, mix the tahini, lemon juice, olive oil, and salt and pepper to taste to form a dressing. Pour most of the dressing on the bottom of a small serving dish. Arrange the zucchini on top of the dressing bed. Season the vegetables with salt and pepper to taste. Drizzle remaining dressing across the top. Serve warm.

Yield: 4 servings

POTATO and
CAULIFLOWER MASH

In an effort to lower the starch content of her family's meals and incorporate additional vegetables, Sheri started using this recipe at home. It has a lighter texture than mashed potatoes and all of the flavor.

1 pound russet potatoes, peeled, rinsed, and cut into 1-inch
    cubes
1 pound cauliflower florets
2 garlic cloves
1/3 cup buttermilk, warmed
3 tablespoons canola margarine
Salt
Freshly ground black pepper
Freshly ground nutmeg
Cayenne pepper, optional

Bring the potatoes, cauliflower, and garlic to boil in a pot of salted water and cook until the potatoes are easily pierced with a fork, about 15 minutes. Drain the vegetables and return them to the pot. Add the buttermilk and margarine and, with an electric mixer on low speed, mash until the mixture is smooth. Season with salt, pepper, nutmeg, and cayenne, if using, to taste. Keep warm until serving.

Yield: 3 cups

RATATOUILLE
CASSEROLE

1 medium eggplant, peeled and cut into julienne
2 zucchini, cut into julienne
1 tablespoon kosher salt, plus additional to taste
1/4 cup canola oil
1 1/2 cups thinly sliced onions
1 cup sliced green bell peppers, optional
2 garlic cloves, minced
Freshly ground black pepper
1 pound firm ripe tomatoes, sliced
3 tablespoons minced fresh parsley
1/2 to 3/4 cup grated Parmesan cheese

Place the eggplant and zucchini strips in a large bowl with 1 tablespoon of the salt and let stand 30 minutes. Rinse and drain the eggplant and zucchini and pat dry.

In a large skillet heat the oil over medium heat and sauté the eggplant and zucchini, stirring, for about 5 minutes. Remove the vegetables from the pan and set aside.

In the same skillet, sauté the onions and bell pepper, if using. Cook and stir until tender. Add the garlic, salt and pepper to taste, and tomatoes. Reduce the heat to low, and cook, stirring, until some of the liquid evaporates.

Preheat the oven to 350°F. Place 1/3 of the tomato mixture in a 2-quart casserole dish, and sprinkle with 1 tablespoon of the parsley. Spread 1/2 of the eggplant-zucchini mixture on top and sprinkle with 1 tablespoon of the parsley. Top with another 1/3 of the tomato mixture. Repeat with the remaining eggplant-zucchini mixture and top with the remaining parsley and the remaining tomato mixture. Cover and bake for 20 minutes. Turn the oven to 400°F, remove the cover, sprinkle with the cheese, and bake, uncovered, for 15 minutes or until tender.
Yield: 6 servings

RIO BRAVO
RICE-STUFFED POBLANOS

This recipe, from the USA Rice Federation website (www.usarice. com), was created by Edwina Gadsby and won the Rice to the Rescue recipe contest in 2004.

6 large poblano peppers
Canola oil
3 cups cooked long-grain white rice
2/3 cup sour cream
1 1/2 cups grated smoked Gouda or cheddar cheese, divided
1 cup frozen corn kernels, thawed
1/3 cup chopped cilantro leaves, plus additional for garnish
Salt
Freshly ground black pepper

Preheat the oven to 400°F. Slit the peppers lengthwise so that they can later be stuffed with rice filling. Carefully remove the loose seeds and veins, keeping the peppers' stems intact. Rub the peppers generously with the oil and place them on a baking sheet.

Combine the rice, the sour cream, 1 cup of the cheese, the corn, and the cilantro in a medium bowl. Season with salt and pepper to taste. Stuff each pepper with about 1/6 of the rice mixture. Sprinkle the stuffed peppers with the remaining cheese. Bake in the oven 20 to 25 minutes, until the peppers are crisp-tender and the filling is heated through. Garnish with cilantro.

Yield: 6 servings

SMOKED GOUDA and
SPINACH RICE CASSEROLE

This recipe by Elise Lalor won the USA Rice Federation's Rice to the Rescue contest in 2005.

Canola oil spray for greasing
3 tablespoons canola oil
1/2 cup finely chopped shallots
2 cups sliced mushrooms
3 cups hot cooked long-grain white rice
1 (10-ounce) package frozen chopped spinach, thawed and
     drained
2 cups grated smoked Gouda cheese, divided
1/2 cup whipping cream
Salt
Freshly ground black pepper

Preheat the broiler and lightly grease a 2-quart casserole dish with the spray.

Heat the oil in a large skillet over medium-high heat. Add the shallots and mushrooms and sauté for about 6 to 8 minutes, or until tender. Add the hot rice, the spinach, 1 1/4 cups of the cheese, and the cream. Stir until the cheese melts and the mixture is heated through.

Spoon the mixture into the prepared casserole dish and sprinkle the remaining cheese over the top. Broil for about 2 minutes or until the cheese melts.

Yield: 6 servings

SPINACH DILL LATKES

This is a great accompaniment to smoked salmon or smoked turkey. This recipe has been adapted from one in the December 1994 issue of *Eating Well* magazine.

Canola oil spray for greasing
1/2 pound (about 4 cups tightly packed) fresh spinach, washed
     and trimmed
2 medium (about 1 pound) russet potatoes, peeled
1/4 cup flour
3 tablespoons chopped fresh dill
3 tablespoons chopped scallions or chives
Salt
Freshly ground black pepper
1 large egg, lightly beaten
1 large egg white, lightly beaten
1 teaspoon canola oil

Place the oven racks at the middle and lowest positions. Preheat the oven to 450°F. Lightly grease 2 baking sheets with the spray.

Add the spinach, with water still on the leaves from washing, to a wok or skillet over high heat. Toss and stir until spinach is wilted. Place the spinach in a colander and, when cool enough to handle, squeeze out the excess water. Chop the spinach coarsely and set aside.

Grate the potatoes and place them in a large bowl. Stir in the flour, dill, scallions, salt and pepper to taste, and reserved spinach. Using two forks, toss to mix well. Stir in the egg, egg white, and oil. Toss again to mix well.

Drop rounded tablespoons of the potato mixture onto the prepared baking sheets and press lightly to form cakes. Bake for 10 minutes, or until the latkes are golden brown on the bottom. Turn them over, switch the position of the baking sheets, and bake for another 5 minutes, or until the latkes are golden brown all over. Transfer the latkes to a platter and serve.
Yield: 20 latkes, or 4 servings

Hint: Latkes may be prepared ahead and stored covered in the refrigerator overnight. Reheat them in an oven at 350°F for 10 minutes.

SWEET and SOUR CARROTS

Even people who dislike cooked carrots will enjoy this dish, which should be made ahead and can be refrigerated for several days. This recipe has been adapted from Sheilah Kaufman's *Sheilah's Fearless, Fussless Cookbook* (Delacorte, 1982).

3 pounds carrots, peeled and cut into 1 1/2-inch rounds
1 (10 3/4-ounce) can tomato soup, undiluted
1 cup cider vinegar
1 cup sugar
1 1/2 cups canola oil
1 teaspoon dry mustard
1 green bell pepper, finely chopped
1 medium onion, finely chopped

The day before serving, bring 4 quarts of salted water to a boil in a large pot. Add the carrots and cook until they can be easily pierced with a fork but not too soft. Drain the carrots well.

In a large glass or nonreactive bowl, combine the soup, vinegar, sugar, oil, mustard, bell pepper, and onion. Add the carrots and mix until they are well coated with the marinade. Cover the bowl and refrigerate overnight or longer if desired.

Yield: 10 to 12 servings

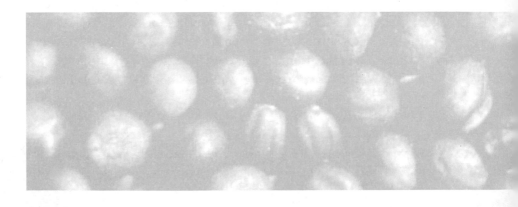

SWEET POTATO BAKE

Sheri has recently made an effort to introduce more sweet potatoes into her family's diet because of their health benefits. This dish is a big hit in that effort and does not include any extra sugar calories. The sweetness of the sweet potatoes and the onions with the herbs leave her kids asking for this side dish again and again. And it is so easy to prepare!

5 pounds sweet potatoes or yams, peeled and cubed into 1/2-
    inch pieces
1 red onion, diced into 1/2-inch pieces
1/3 cup canola oil
2 tablespoons herbes de Province
Salt
Freshly ground black pepper

Preheat the oven to 375°F. Mix all of the ingredients in a large bowl and pour them into a baking dish. Bake uncovered for 45 minutes to 1 hour, or until the potato edges become brown and crisp.
Yield: 8 to 10 servings

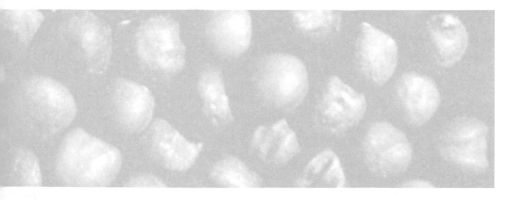

CHAPTER 9

Breads, Muffins, and More

APPLESAUCE LOAF

Canola oil spray for greasing
Flour for dusting
1/2 cup canola oil
1 cup firmly packed brown sugar
1 large egg
1 cup unsweetened applesauce
1 1/2 cups whole wheat flour
1/4 teaspoon salt
1 teaspoon baking soda
1 teaspoon ground cinnamon
1/4 teaspoon ground cloves
1/2 teaspoon allspice
1 cup raisins

Preheat the oven to 350°F. Grease a 9x5-inch loaf pan with the spray and dust with flour. Using an electric mixer, combine the oil, sugar, and egg. Add the applesauce. Reduce the speed to low, add the whole wheat flour, salt, baking soda, spices, and raisins, and mix until just combined. Be careful not to overbeat. Pour the batter into the prepared loaf pan and bake for 35 to 40 minutes.

Yield: 12 servings

CARAMELIZED ONION
FOCACCIA

Canola oil spray for greasing
2 tablespoons canola oil
2 cups bread flour
1 tablespoon sugar
1 teaspoon kosher salt
1 1/2 teaspoons bread yeast
1/4 cup canola margarine
4 large Myna or Vidalia onions, sliced thin
3/4 cup grated Mozzarella cheese
3 tablespoons grated Parmesan cheese

Lightly grease a cookie sheet with the spray and set aside.

In a large bowl, combine 3/4 cup water, oil, flour, sugar, salt, and yeast. Mix well.

Place the dough on a lightly floured work surface and pat into a circle. Place on the prepared cookie sheet, cover with a clean kitchen towel, and let rise for about 30 minutes, or until almost double in size. Meanwhile prepare the onion topping. Melt the margarine in a large skillet, and sauté the onions until they are browned and caramelized, about 25 to 30 minutes, stirring occasionally. Remove from heat.

Preheat the oven to 400°F. Make deep depressions in the dough with your finger at 1-inch intervals. Spread the onion topping over the dough. Sprinkle the cheeses over the top and bake for 15 to 18 minutes, or until the edges are golden brown. Remove the bread from the cookie sheet and place on a wire rack. Let cool for only a minute or two before serving. Cut in wedges and serve warm.

Yield: 12 servings

Hint: Myna and Vidalia onions have a higher sugar content than regular yellow onions and caramelize better.

CHOCOLATE CHIP
BANANA BREAD

It always seems like we have ripe bananas sitting on the counter: Does this sound familiar? This recipe was quickly created when the Coleman family discovered how the flavors of bananas and chocolate go together like a hand in a glove. Enjoy!

Canola oil spray
1/3 cup canola oil
1 cup sugar
3 eggs, beaten
3 cups flour
4 to 5 medium bananas, mashed
1/2 cup chocolate chips
2/3 cup buttermilk
1 1/2 teaspoons baking soda
1/2 teaspoon salt
1/2 cup chopped walnuts or pecans, optional

Preheat the oven to 325°F. Grease a 9x5-inch loaf pan with the spray. In a large bowl, combine the oil, sugar, eggs, flour, bananas, chocolate chips, buttermilk, baking soda, salt, and nuts, if using, and stir until just blended. Pour the batter into the pan and bake about one hour, until the top is lightly golden brown and the sides pull away from edges of pan. Remove the pan from oven and cool. Slice the bread and serve with canola margarine.
Yield: 10 to 12 servings

GRAPE and CRANBERRY TEA BREAD

Grapes and cranberries are a lovely combination. This recipe is courtesy of the California Table Grape Commission.

Canola oil spray for greasing
2 1/2 cups flour, plus more for dusting
3/4 cup sugar
3 teaspoons baking powder
1 teaspoon salt
1/4 cup canola oil
1 cup low-fat sour cream
1/4 cup low-fat milk
1 large egg, beaten
2 teaspoons lemon zest
1/2 cup chopped walnuts
1/2 cup chopped dried cranberries
1 1/2 cups halved fresh California seedless grapes

Preheat the oven to 350°F. Grease 2 9x5-inch loaf pans or 4 mini loaf pans with the spray and lightly flour the bottoms of each greased pan. Combine 2 1/2 cups of the flour, the sugar, baking powder, salt, oil, sour cream, milk, egg, lemon zest, walnuts, and cranberries, and mix well. Gently fold in the grapes, and pour the batter into the prepared pans. Bake for 40 to 45 minutes or until a cake tester inserted in the center comes out clean. Cool for 5 minutes, and then turn out onto wire rack. Cool completely before slicing.

Yield: 2 loaves or 4 small loaves

HERBED CORN
MUFFINS

These muffins are a great accompaniment to many dishes. If you'd like, you can omit the rosemary and have the muffins topped with honey and canola margarine for breakfast.

Canola oil spray
1 cup flour
1 cup coarse yellow cornmeal
1/2 cup sugar
1 1/2 teaspoons baking powder
1/4 teaspoon baking soda
1/4 teaspoon salt
1 teaspoon finely chopped fresh rosemary, plus additional leaves
    for garnish
1 cup plus 2 tablespoons fresh corn kernels, divided
1 cup buttermilk
1 large egg, lightly beaten
1/4 cup canola oil

Preheat the oven to 375°F. Lightly grease a standard 12-cup muffin tin with the spray.

Whisk together the flour, cornmeal, sugar, baking powder, baking soda, salt, rosemary, and 1 cup of the corn. Combine the buttermilk, egg, and oil in a small bowl. Add the buttermilk mixture to the flour mixture and stir until just combined. Spoon the batter into the muffin cups, filling three-quarters full. Top with the remaining corn and a few rosemary leaves.

Bake until the muffin tops are golden and a cake tester inserted in the center comes out clean, 15 to 17 minutes. Let the muffins cool in the tin on a wire rack for 5 minutes. Then turn out the muffins onto the rack. Serve the muffins warm or at room temperature. They can be stored in an airtight container for up to 2 days.
Yield: 2 dozen

HONEY DOUGHNUTS

These doughnuts are like the Greek treats loukoumathes. Almost any variety of honey will be good in these, but Sheilah especially likes the apple-peach blossom honey from Toigo Orchards in Pennsylvania. She first tasted these doughnuts at a Slow Foods dinner at Clyde's Restaurant in Washington, D.C. They were prepared by pastry chef Travis Olson, who kindly provided this recipe.

2 cups luke-warm milk
2 tablespoons sugar
1/2 teaspoon salt
2 large eggs
2 ounces butter, melted
4 cups flour
2 teaspoons dried yeast
Canola oil for frying
Honey
Cinnamon-sugar, optional

In a medium bowl, combine the milk, sugar, salt, eggs, and melted butter. Stir in the flour and yeast. Whisk or beat thoroughly for 3 to 4 minutes. The batter will be soft. Cover the bowl and let the batter rise for 2 hours.

Heat a pot of canola oil to 375°F for deep frying. Stir the batter gently to knock some of the air out of it. Use 2 soupspoons to gently drop tablespoon-size bits of dough into the oil. It helps to dip the spoons in the oil before dipping them into the batter. Fry several doughnuts at a time, but don't crowd the pot. The doughnuts are ready when they are deep golden brown in color. Immediately transfer the fried doughnuts to a mixing bowl with a little honey in it. Toss to coat the doughnuts. If desired, toss the honey-coated doughnuts in cinnamon-sugar.

Yield: 48 small doughnuts

KERRY'S DELICIOUS BISCUITS

This tasty biscuit makes a nice accompaniment to soups and salads. This recipe has been adapted from one in Kerry Dunnington's *This Book Cooks*.

1 package active dry yeast
1/4 cup plus 1 teaspoon sugar
4 cups all-purpose flour
1/2 cup wheat flour
1/2 cup wheat germ
1 teaspoon baking powder
1 teaspoon baking soda
1 teaspoon salt
1/2 cup canola oil
2 cups low-fat buttermilk
Canola oil spray for greasing

In a medium bowl, combine the yeast and 1 teaspoon of the sugar. Add 1/2 cup warm water and stir until the yeast and sugar have dissolved; allow to proof for about 5 minutes.

In a large mixing bowl, combine the flours, wheat germ, 1/4 cup sugar, baking powder, baking soda, and salt. Slowly drizzle oil over flour mixture and toss with a fork until mixture resembles coarse meal. Add the yeast mixture and buttermilk. Stir until moist. Cover and chill for 1 hour or overnight.

Preheat the oven to 450°F. Grease a baking sheet with the spray.

Turn the chilled dough out onto a heavily floured surface and knead several times. Roll into a 1/2-inch thickness and cut with a round 2- to 3-inch cookie or biscuit cutter. Arrange the biscuits on the prepared baking sheet and bake for 11 to 13 minutes or until golden.

Yield: 24 biscuits

PARMESAN SKILLET
CORNBREAD

This recipe is easy to throw together and bake. If you don't have a cast-iron skillet, you can also use a stove-top frying pan that is suitable for baking or a coated cast-iron baking dish. Serve this cornbread as an accompaniment to your Italian dishes.

1 1/4 cups whole grain pastry flour
1 cup stone-ground yellow cornmeal
1 tablespoon sugar
1 tablespoon baking powder
1/2 teaspoon baking soda
1/2 teaspoon salt
1 large egg
2 teaspoons tomato paste
1 1/2 teaspoons finely chopped fresh rosemary
1/4 cup plus 1 tablespoon canola oil
1 cup milk
1 cup grated Parmesan cheese
1/2 cup Kalamata olives, pitted and coarsely chopped
1/2 teaspoon hot pepper sauce

Preheat the oven to 450°F. Place a 10-inch cast-iron skillet or 9-inch ovenproof skillet (do not use nonstick) on the center rack in the oven. Heat for 30 minutes.

In a large bowl, whisk the flour, cornmeal, sugar, baking powder, baking soda, and salt. Whisk the egg, tomato paste, and rosemary in a medium bowl to blend. Whisk 1/4 cup of the oil and then the milk into the egg mixture. Add the egg mixture to the dry ingredients, and stir the batter until just blended. Stir in the cheese and olives.

Remove the skillet from the oven. Add the remaining canola oil to the skillet and swirl to coat the bottom and sides. Spoon the batter into the hot skillet. Place the skillet in the oven and reduce the temperature to 400°F. Bake the bread until it is golden brown and a cake tester inserted in the center comes out clean, about 22 minutes. Cool for 5 minutes and then invert the bread onto a wire rack. Turn the bread over. Serve warm or at room temperature.

Yield: 8 servings

POPPY SEED BREAD

When Norma and Bob Morris's daughters graduated from high school, they moved to Aspen for a few years and then to Carbondale, where they opened a four-bedroom bed and breakfast, the Ambiance Inn (www.ambianceinn.com, ambianceinn@aol.com). Eighteen years later, they are still enjoying Carbondale. Their guests love this bread.

Canola oil spray for greasing
3 cups flour
1/2 teaspoon salt
1 1/2 teaspoons baking powder
4 tablespoons poppy seeds
2 3/4 cups sugar
1 1/2 cup canola oil
3 large eggs
1 1/2 teaspoons vanilla
3 teaspoons almond extract
1 1/2 cups milk
3/4 cup freshly squeezed orange juice

Preheat the oven to 375°F. Grease 2 9x5-inch loaf pans or 3 mini loaf pans with the spray. In a large bowl, combine the flour, salt, baking powder, and poppy seeds and set aside.

Using an electric mixer, cream 2 cups of the sugar, the oil, the eggs, the vanilla, and 1 1/2 teaspoons of the almond extract in a medium bowl. On low speed, add the dry ingredients to the sugar mixture alternately with the milk, ending with the dry ingredients. Place the mixture in the prepared pans and bake for 1 hour, or until a cake tester inserted in the center of the loaves comes out clean.

While the bread is cooking, combine the orange juice, the remaining sugar, and the remaining almond extract. Drizzle this mixture over the hot bread right after you remove it from the oven.
Yield: 2 loaves

PUMPKIN RIBBON
BREAD

Ginnie Manuel used to live in Ramsen, New York, where her pumpkin bread recipe (adapted below) won the city's annual baking contest several years ago.

Canola oil spray for greasing
Flour for dusting

The filling:
2 (3-ounce) packages cream cheese, softened
1/3 cup sugar
1 tablespoon flour
1 large egg
2 teaspoons orange zest

The bread:
1 cup cooked pureed pumpkin
1/2 cup canola oil
2 large eggs
1 1/2 cups sugar
1/2 teaspoon salt
1/2 teaspoon ground cloves
1/2 teaspoon ground cinnamon
1 2/3 cups flour
1 teaspoon baking soda
1 cup chopped pecans

Preheat the oven to 325°F. Grease 2 9x5-inch loaf pans with the spray and dust both with flour.

To make the filling, beat the cream cheese, sugar, and flour in a small bowl. Add the egg and mix to blend well. Stir in the orange zest and set aside.

To make the bread, mix the pumpkin, oil, and eggs in a medium bowl until smooth. Add the remaining ingredients in order given, and mix until well blended. Pour one-quarter of the batter into each of the two prepared pans. Divide the cream cheese mixture between the two pans, spreading carefully over the batter. Top with the remaining batter to cover the filling. Bake for 45 minutes to 1 hour, or until a cake tester inserted in the center of each loaf comes out clean.

Cool the loaves for 10 minutes on a wire rack before removing them from the pans. Store in the refrigerator.
Yield: 2 loaves

SOFT GRANOLA

Sheri came up with this recipe after sampling soft granola in Big Sky, Montana, her family's home away from home. This recipe can be served either warm or cold as a breakfast cereal. And if you don't mind sticky fingers, it's also a great snack to take along on a hike. Use your imagination when considering dried fruit and nut combinations—they will all turn out delicious!

3 cups rolled oats
1 cup sliced almonds, pine nuts, chopped walnuts, chopped
　　pecan, or a combination of all 4
1 cup dried cranberries, dried cherries, dried blueberries, or a
　　combination of all 3
1/3 cup canola oil
1/2 cup honey
1 tablespoon vanilla powder

In a large mixing bowl, combine the rolled outs with the nuts and dried fruit. Mix gently and set aside.

In small saucepan over low heat, combine the oil and honey and gently stir for 3 minutes, until mixture is smooth and runny. Remove from heat and pour over the oat, fruit, and nut mixture. Add the vanilla powder. Stir until the oats are evenly coated with the honey mixture. Place in airtight container and store for up to 1 week.
Yield: 8 to 10 servings

Hint: Sheri prefers to use Bob's Red Mill brand grains and flours for her recipes.

STONE-GROUND
WHOLE WHEAT BREAD

This healthy bread is easy to make. Nur Ilkin, the wife of the U.S. ambassador to Turkey, taught Sheilah this recipe when they were writing *A Taste of Turkish Cuisine* (Hippocrene Books, 2002). Nur loves baking this bread and serving it to her friends. You will too.

1 tablespoon dry yeast dissolved in 2 tablespoons warm water
1/4 cup canola oil
1 tablespoon honey
3 1/2 cups stone-ground whole wheat
1/4 cup milk, at room temperature
1 to 1 1/2 teaspoons salt
Canola oil for greasing

In a large bowl, combine the yeast and water, oil, honey, wheat, milk, salt, and 1 1/3 cups water, mixing well until a dough is formed. This can also be done in a mixer using a dough hook. If the dough is too sticky, add a little more flour. If you are going to knead the dough by hand, transfer the dough to a lightly greased work surface and knead for 6 to 8 minutes. If using the mixer, knead the dough for 5 minutes with the dough hook.

Lightly grease a bowl with the spray. Place the dough in the greased bowl, cover with a towel, and let sit in a warm place until it doubles in size, about 1 hour. Then place the dough on a lightly floured surface and punch it down lightly. Place the dough in a lightly greased 9x5-inch loaf pan, cover with a kitchen towel, and let it rise again for another hour.

Preheat the oven to 350°F. Bake the bread for 40 minutes. If the top gets too dark before the baking is done, cover it with a piece of aluminum foil.

Yield: 1 loaf

ZUCCHINI BREAD

Sheilah generally prefers sweets to bread, but this bread tastes like cake. At times she even serves it as cake—and thereby tricks her husband and kids into eating their vegetables for dessert. The zucchini makes this bread delightfully moist. This recipe is adapted from one in Sheilah's *Simply Irresistible: Easy, Elegant, Fearless, Fussless Cooking.*

Canola oil spray for greasing
3 cups flour, plus additional for dusting
2 small zucchini
3 large eggs
1 cup canola oil
2 cups sugar
2 teaspoons vanilla extract
1 teaspoon salt
1 teaspoon baking soda
1 tablespoon ground cinnamon
1/4 teaspoon baking powder

Preheat the oven to 350°F. Grease 2 9x5-inch loaf pans with the spray and dust both with flour. Wash and dry the zucchini but do not peel them. Cut them into thick slices and grate the slices in a food processor. Set the zucchini aside.

In a large bowl, beat the eggs until light and frothy with an electric mixer at medium speed. Add the oil, sugar, grated zucchini, and vanilla and beat well. Sift the 3 cups flour, the salt, baking soda, cinnamon, and baking powder onto a sheet of waxed paper and add it to the bowl, mixing well. Pour the batter into the prepared pans and bake for 1 hour.

Cool the loaves in their pans on a wire rack for 30 minutes; then turn the loaves out onto the wire rack to cool completely. Wrap the loaves in aluminum foil and refrigerate for several hours for easier slicing. The loaves may be frozen.
Yield: 2 loaves

SWEET ONION ROLLS

This recipe was originally published in *When the Kaiser Roll Was King* by Marive Korman (Red Rock Press, www.RedRockPress. com). To make these sweet onion rolls, which are like those Marvin's father made in his bakery every Friday, follow the dough preparation for Uncle Menashe's Magic Challah (see page 172) through the point at which you are ready to shape the dough into braids. These rolls are best served within an hour or two after they are retrieved from the oven. And Marvin says, "They require no adornments, no butter, no jam, nothing!"

Canola oil spray for greasing
1 recipe Uncle Menashe's Magic Challah dough (see page 172)
3 large onions, finely chopped (about 2 cups)
1 tablespoon canola oil, plus additional as needed
1 egg, beaten
3 tablespoons poppy seeds

Grease 2 cookie sheets with the spray.

After you have kneaded the Challah dough, divide it into quarters and then divide each section into quarters again, so that you have 16 pieces. Shape each piece into a round ball and place the balls on the prepared cookie sheets, eight balls to a sheet. Make sure you leave at least three inches between each ball. Press the dough down with your knuckles to make a hollow in the center of each ball. Cover with a kitchen towel and let the rolls rise in a warm spot for 20 to 25 minutes, or until they have doubled in size.

While you wait for the rolls to rise, prepare the onions. In a skillet, sauté the onions in the oil, adding an additional two tablespoons of oil if the pan gets dry. Cook until the onions are translucent but not brown. Remove the onions from the pan and set aside.

Place a deep-sided empty pan in the oven on the bottom rack and preheat the oven to 450°F. When the rolls have doubled in size, punch them down with your knuckles again. Each roll should be about 4 inches in diameter. Fill each hollow center with two tablespoons of cooked onions. Brush each roll with the beaten egg and sprinkle a teaspoon of poppy seeds on each.

Add 4 cups of cold water to the heated pan at the bottom of your oven to create steam. (Use caution when doing this. Wear baking mitts and be sure the steam doesn't hit your face.) Turn down the heat of the oven to 375°F and place the rolls into the oven. Bake for about 20 to 25 minutes or until the rolls are a golden brown. Remove the rolls from the oven and cool on a rack for about an hour.

HERBED GARLIC BREAD

This recipe has been adapted from one on the Hellmann's website, www.hellmanns.com.

1/4 cup canola oil or canola margarine
2 tablespoons minced fresh parsley
1 1/2 teaspoons minced fresh basil, or 1/2 teaspoon dried basil
1 garlic clove, minced
1/4 cup grated Parmesan cheese
1 (8-ounce) loaf French bread, sliced in half lengthwise

Preheat your broiler or grill to medium heat.

In a small pan over low heat, combine the oil, parsley, basil, and garlic. Heat, stirring, until the oil is warm. Stir in the Parmesan cheese. Grill the bread cut side down or broil cut side up for 2 minutes, until slightly toasted. Brush the cut side with the oil mixture. Grill or broil for an additional 1 to 2 minutes

Yield: 4 servings

UNCLE MENASHE'S
MAGIC CHALLAH

This recipe was originally published in *When the Kaiser Roll Was King* by Marvin Korman (Red Rock Press, www.RedRockPress.com). "On Fridays," Marvin writes, "in addition to the regular assortment of breads and rolls, my father's bakery would prepare Challah, easily the best tasting bread in the world. Am I hearing any arguments? . . . My great uncle Menashe, who was our master Challah baker, taught the other bread bakers how to prepare a Challah with care; it was he who showed me that baking was more than a craft or even an art—it was magic. . . . The Challah was served as part of the Friday evening Sabbath dinners. My father would also send a large Challah about three feet in length to our local synagogue every Friday. . . . Today, Challah are everywhere, and are served as French Toast in countless Sunday brunches. I am always amused when strips of grilled bacon, along with the kiwis and strawberries, are served with it. Uncle Menashe surely would have rolled his eyes at that!"

3 (1/4-ounce) packages dry yeast
1/2 cup plus 1 tablespoon sugar
3 tablespoons canola margarine
4 eggs
1 tablespoon kosher salt
5 1/2 to 6 1/2 cups bread flour
Canola oil spray for greasing
1 tablespoon poppy seeds

In a large bowl, add the yeast and 1 tablespoon of the sugar to 1 1/2 cups warm water. Cover with a kitchen towel and place on top of the stove. Turn on the oven to the lowest level of heat to warm the air around the bowl.

While the yeast is proofing, melt the margarine in a small saucepan. Remove from heat.

Beat 3 eggs in a small bowl. Add the salt and the remaining sugar, and then add the egg mixture to the margarine. When the surface of the water and yeast mixture is covered with a bubbly skin (this indicates that the yeast has proofed), add the margarine mixture to the yeast mixture and stir.

Add 5 to 5 1/2 cups of the flour, one cup at a time to the liquid mixture. Mix well with a wooden spoon after each addition. When all of the flour is absorbed and you have a nice, soft ball of dough, turn the dough out onto a large wooden kneading board. Add handfuls of flour as you knead, folding, turning, and pushing down on the dough with your hands until you have a soft but firm mound. Grease a second large bowl with the spray. Place the dough into the bowl and turn to coat. Cover the bowl with a kitchen towel or, if you are eager to see it rise, with clear polyethylene wrap. Place the bowl back on top of the stove for about an hour or so, until the dough has doubled in size.

Preheat the oven to 400°F.

Sprinkle the kneading board with more flour, then take the dough from the bowl and repeatedly punch it down on the board. Keep kneading for five or ten minutes until you've removed all of the air from the dough and its surface is not sticky.

Divide the dough in half and divide each half into three parts. Take one of the sections and roll it between the palms of your hands, creating a small rope of dough. Place this small rope onto your board; using the palms of both hands, extend the size of the rope to about 12 inches in length. Do this for all six pieces of dough. Set aside three of the pieces. Lay the remaining three side by side, pinching the ends together at one end; then braid them together. Repeat the process with the other three ropes for the second Challah. Place each loaf onto a large, nonstick cookie sheet (the largest you can fit into your oven, one above the other) that has been greased with the spray. Place each sheet on the top of the stove for 25 or 30 minutes, or until the loaves have doubled in size. Lightly beat the remaining egg. Remove the sheets from the top of the stove and brush gently with the beaten egg. Sprinkle poppy seeds on top of each loaf.

Place the loaves in the oven. Check the loaves after 25 to 30 minutes. The Challah should be nicely browned and glowing, dark but not burned on the bottom. Remove from the oven and cool on a wire rack for an hour or two.

Hint: If you are frightened by the prospect of braiding the loaves, they can be baked in individual loaf pans. Simply place three balls of dough side by side into two loaf pans. Let the dough rise to just below the tops of the pans, brush with the egg, and sprinkle with poppy seeds. The baking time may be a few minutes longer, but you will be able to tell when they are done. Remove them from the pans and cool on a wire rack.

SHERI'S FAVORITE
PUMPKIN BREAD

The smell of cinnamon and nutmeg wafts through the house as this bread bakes, letting you know that fall has arrived.

Canola oil spray for greasing
3 1/2 cups flour
2 teaspoons baking soda
1 1/2 teaspoons salt
2 teaspoons ground cinnamon
1 teaspoon ground nutmeg
3 cups sugar
1 cup canola oil
4 eggs
2 cups canned pumpkin

Preheat the oven to 350°F. Grease 2 9x5-inch loaf pans with the spray. Mix all of the remaining ingredients in a large bowl. Pour the batter into the prepared loaf pans and bake for 1 hour and 15 minutes. Cool on wire racks.

Yield: 2 loaves

The following spreads will be delicious on your favorite baked buns and breads. The raspberry and maple spreads are also great on pancakes.

HERBED SPREAD

1/2 cup canola margarine
1 tablespoon minced fresh parsley
1/2 teaspoon minced garlic
1 teaspoon Italian seasoning
1/4 teaspoon crushed red pepper

In a small bowl, combine all of the ingredients. Serve immediately or refrigerate until needed.
Yield: 1/2 cup

RASPBERRY SPREAD

1/2 cup canola margarine
1/3 cup fresh raspberries
2 tablespoons confectioners' sugar
Dash lemon juice

In a small bowl, combine all of the ingredients. Serve immediately or refrigerate until needed.
Yield: 3/4 cup

SPICED MAPLE SPREAD

1/2 cup canola margarine
1/4 cup maple syrup
1/2 teaspoon ground cinnamon
1 teaspoon orange zest

In a small bowl, combine all of the ingredients. Serve immediately or refrigerate until needed.
Yield: 3/4 cup

CHAPTER 10

Desserts—
Cakes

_____ **CARAMEL SAUCE**

Use this recipe on top of your favorite spice cake or ice cream or on
the fried banana recipe (see page 201).

1 1/2 cups brown sugar
3 tablespoons canola margarine
1 cup whipping cream

In a heavy large saucepan over medium-low heat, combine the sugar
and 1/2 cup water, stirring until the sugar dissolves. Increase the heat
and boil without stirring until the syrup is deep amber, about 12 minutes.
Remove the pan from heat. Whisk in the canola margarine. Gradually
pour in the cream; the mixture will bubble up. Return the pan to low
heat and stir until the sauce is smooth. Pour into a bowl. Cool to
lukewarm. Store in the refrigerator for up to 2 days. Rewarm before
using.
Yield: 2 cups

CHOCOLATE
PORT SAUCE

If you can let this sauce last long enough to make it out of the pan, it is wonderful on top of your favorite chocolate cake or a little vanilla ice cream.

3/4 cup whipping cream
1/4 cup whole milk
1/4 cup canola margarine
8 ounces semisweet chocolate, chopped
1/4 cup tawny port

Bring the cream, milk, and margarine to a simmer in small heavy saucepan over medium heat. Remove the saucepan from heat and add the chopped chocolate. Whisk the mixture until smooth. Stir in the tawny port. Serve immediately or store covered in the refrigerator for up to 2 days. Before serving warm over medium-low heat.
Yield: 2 cups

BUTTERMILK PRUNE CAKE

This recipe is courtesy of Carol Steig, who won first place in the Northern Canola Growers Association's Canola Cook Off in 2005.

The cake:
Canola oil spray for greasing
1 cup canola oil
1/4 cup sugar
1/2 cup buttermilk
3 large eggs
2 cups flour
1 teaspoon salt
1 teaspoon baking soda
1 1/2 teaspoons ground cinnamon
1 1/2 teaspoons ground nutmeg
1 cup chopped prunes
1 cup chopped pecans, toasted

The sauce:
3/4 cup sugar
1/2 cup buttermilk
1 teaspoon baking soda
1/4 cup canola margarine, melted

Preheat the oven to 350°F. Grease a 13x9-inch baking pan with the spray.

In a large mixing bowl, blend the oil, sugar, buttermilk, and eggs until smooth. Add the flour, salt, baking soda, cinnamon, and nutmeg and mix well. Fold in the prunes and nuts. Spread mixture into the prepared pan and bake for 40 minutes, or until a cake tester inserted in the center comes out clean.

When the cake is done, remove it from oven and, using a fork, prick holes all over the surface of the cake. Combine the sugar, buttermilk, baking soda, and margarine in a small mixing bowl and whisk until the sugar and baking soda have dissolved. Pour over the warm cake.

This dessert can be served warm or cold. Store in a refrigerator.
Yield: 12 servings

CHERRY
BREAKFAST BAKE

Sheri first had this dish on a chilly Wisconsin morning a few years back while she was visiting her aunt Susie. This recipe is flexible: it can be used at any meal or as a dessert and any fruit pie filling can be substituted for the cherry pie filling.

The cake:
Canola oil spray for greasing
1/2 cup canola margarine
2 cups flour
1 cup sugar
2 teaspoons baking powder
1/2 teaspoon salt
2 large eggs, beaten
1/2 cup milk
1 (15-ounce) can cherry pie filling

The glaze:
1 cup confectioners' sugar
2 tablespoons canola margarine, melted
2 tablespoons milk

Preheat the oven to 350°F. Grease a 13x9-inch baking dish with the spray.

Mix the margarine, flour, sugar, baking powder, and salt together until crumbly. Remove half of the mixture to another bowl and set aside for the topping.

To the original bowl add the eggs and milk until incorporated. Pour the batter into the prepared baking dish. Dollop spoonfuls of cherry pie filling on top of the batter. Don't worry if the dollops are not evenly distributed. Sprinkle with the reserved topping. Bake for 45 minutes.

While the cake is baking, combine the glaze ingredients in a small bowl. Whisk until the sugar has dissolved.

Remove the cake from the oven and drizzle with the glaze.
Yield: 12 servings

CHOCOLATE PUDDING CAKE

This cake bakes with its own pudding inside. It is truly an impressive dessert that any chocolate lover will be unable to resist. The ice cream provides a nice contrast to the chocolate.

Canola cooking spray for greasing
1 cup sifted flour
1/2 teaspoon baking soda
2 teaspoons baking powder
1/4 teaspoon cinnamon
1/4 teaspoon salt
1 cup sugar, divided
1/2 cup cocoa powder, divided
1/2 cup milk
1 teaspoon vanilla extract
1/4 cup canola oil
1/2 cup packed dark brown sugar
1/4 cup brandy
Vanilla ice cream, optional

Preheat the oven to 350°F. Grease a 9-inch deep-dish pie pan with the spray.

In a large bowl, mix together the flour, baking soda, baking powder, cinnamon, salt, 3/4 cup of the sugar, and 1/4 cup of the cocoa. Stir in the milk, vanilla, and oil. Mix thoroughly by hand or with an electric mixer. The batter will be very thick. Using a rubber spatula, transfer the batter into the prepared pan. Sprinkle the top of the batter with the brown sugar, then sprinkle on the remaining cocoa, and lastly sprinkle on the remaining sugar. Pour 3/4 cup hot water and then the brandy over the top.

Bake for 25 to 30 minutes, or until the top begins to bubble and the cake begins to pull away from the sides of the pan. Cool the cake on a wire rack. Then cover and refrigerate. If desired, serve with a scoop of vanilla ice cream.

Yield: 6 servings

CHOCOLATE
CARROT CAKE

This recipe is guaranteed to give you a Rocky Mountain high! Norma and Bob Morris have been running the Ambiance Inn in Carbondale, a small mountain community at the base of the Sopris Mountains, for eighteen years. This recipe has been a favorite among their bed and breakfast guests.

The cake:

Canola oil spray for greasing
2 cups flour, plus additional for dusting
1 1/2 cups sugar
1 cup canola oil
1/2 cup freshly squeezed orange juice
1/4 cup cocoa powder
2 teaspoons baking soda
1 teaspoon salt
1 teaspoon ground cinnamon
1 teaspoon vanilla extract
4 large eggs, at room temperature
2 cups grated carrots
1 (4-ounce) package shredded coconut

The glaze:

1 cup confectioners' sugar
2 tablespoons frozen orange juice concentrate, thawed, plus
　　　additional as needed
1/4 teaspoon orange zest, optional

Preheat the oven to 350°F. Grease a Bundt pan with the spray and then dust with flour.

In a large bowl, mix the 2 cups flour, sugar, oil, orange juice, cocoa, baking soda, salt, cinnamon, vanilla, and eggs with an electric mixer at low speed. Increase the speed to high and beat for 2 minutes. Stir in the carrots and coconut, mix well, and spoon the mixture into the prepared pan. Bake for 50 to 55 minutes or until a cake tester inserted in the center comes out clean. Cool on a wire rack for 10 to 15 minutes and remove the cake from the pan.

While the cake is cooling, prepare the glaze. Place the sugar in a large bowl and mix with the orange juice and zest, if using. If needed, add more orange juice, a few drops at a time, until the mixture reaches glaze consistency. Pour the glaze over the cake.

Yield: 10 servings

Hint: For this recipe, use large eggs at room temperature. At room temperature more egg white will release from the shell when you crack the egg, and this will yield a lighter, fluffier batter.

CHOCOLATE MOUSSE CAKE

This recipe, from Sheilah Kaufman's *Simply Irresistible: Easy, Elegant, Fearless, Fussless Cooking*, is not as hard as it looks and well worth the effort! The chocolate cake is a good basic cake to make without the filling.

The cake:

1/2 cup sifted unsweetened cocoa powder
1 3/4 cups cake flour
1 3/4 cups sugar
1 1/2 teaspoons baking soda
Pinch of salt
1/2 cup canola oil
7 large egg yolks
2 teaspoons vanilla extract
8 large egg whites, at room temperature
1/2 teaspoon cream of tartar

The chocolate mousse:

3 cups heavy cream
1 1/2 cups sifted confectioners' sugar
3/4 cup unsweetened cocoa powder
1 1/2 teaspoons vanilla extract
1/2 teaspoon rum
Pinch of salt
1 teaspoon unflavored gelatin

Preheat oven to 325°F. In a small saucepan, bring 3/4 cup water to a boil over high heat.

Place the cocoa in a small bowl and add the boiling water. Stir until smooth. Cool the cocoa for 20 minutes.

Sift the flour, sugar, baking soda, and salt into a large bowl. Make a well in the center and pour in the oil, yolks, vanilla, and cooled cocoa mixture. Beat with an electric mixer or spoon just until smooth.

Place the egg whites in a large bowl. Sprinkle cream of tartar over the egg whites and beat with an electric mixer at high speed until stiff peaks form.

Pour the batter over the egg whites and, with a rubber spatula, gently fold the batter into the whites. Turn the mixture into an ungreased 10-inch tube pan. Bake for 60 minutes. Cool completely.

To prepare the mousse, pour the cream into a large bowl and refrigerate until it is very cold, about 30 minutes. Add the sugar, cocoa, vanilla, rum, and salt to the chilled cream and beat with an electric mixer until stiff. Refrigerate.

Sprinkle the gelatin over 2 tablespoons cold water in a small pot. Heat the pot over a slightly larger saucepan of hot water and stir until the gelatin dissolves. Let it cool.

To fill, cut across the cake horizontally 1 inch down from the top of the cake. Set the top of the cake aside. With a sharp knife, outline a well in the bottom part of the cake leaving a 3/4-inch thick wall around the center hole and along the outside. With a spoon, carefully dig out the cake from this area, leaving at least 1 inch at the base. Save 1 1/2 cups of the removed cake, crumble into smaller pieces, and set aside.

Place 2 1/2 cups of the chocolate mousse in a small bowl. Fold in the cooled gelatin. Fill the well in the cake with this mixture. Replace the top of the cake. Mix 1/2 cup of the chocolate mousse with the reserved crumbled cake, and fill in the hole in the center of the cake with this mixture. Frost the top and sides of the cake with the remaining mousse. Refrigerate until chilled.

Yield: 10 to 12 servings

Hint: When baking cakes, use pans that are 2 to 3 inches deep. Pans that are shallower allow the cake to bake up to the top of the pan and continue to rise into a bump or crown in the middle.

CRANBERRY
PUDDING CAKE

This is a favorite of Sheri's that has been handed down in her family for four generations. Even though she's replaced the butter—which is full of saturated fat—with canola margarine, her family still raves!

The cake:
Canola oil spray for greasing
1/4 cup canola margarine
1/2 cup sugar
1 large egg
1/2 cup milk
1 teaspoon baking powder
1 cup flour
1/4 teaspoon salt
1 1/2 cups chopped fresh cranberries

The sauce:
1/2 cup canola margarine
1/2 cup confectioners' sugar
3/4 cup heavy cream
1 teaspoon vanilla extract
Rum, optional

Preheat the oven to 350°F. Grease an 8x8-inch glass baking dish with the spray.

In a large bowl, combine the margarine, sugar, egg, milk, baking powder, flour, salt, and cranberries and mix with an electric mixer until just moistened. Pour the batter into the prepared baking dish. Bake for 35 minutes, or until a cake tester inserted in the center comes out clean.

While the cake is baking, heat the margarine, sugar, cream, vanilla, and rum to taste in a saucepan over medium-low heat, stirring until the sugar is dissolved. Keep warm.

When the cake is done, remove it from the oven. Let it cool slightly. Slice it into 9 equal pieces and place the pieces on dessert plates or in bowls. Serve topped with the sauce.

Yield: 9 servings

CRANBERRY
UPSIDE-DOWN CAKE

One of Sheri's favorite fruits from Wisconsin is the cranberry. Many of her cake, salad, and cookie recipes contain this beloved tart berry. Enjoy this recipe as a breakfast cake, dessert, or afternoon brunch cake.

1 1/2 cups whole grain pastry flour
1 1/2 teaspoons baking powder
1 teaspoon baking soda
1/2 teaspoon ground cinnamon
1/4 teaspoon salt
2/3 cup packed brown sugar
1/3 cup canola margarine
1 1/4 cups cranberries
1/2 cup chopped pecans
1/3 cup canola oil
3/4 cup sugar
2 eggs
1 teaspoon vanilla extract
1 cup sour cream

Preheat the oven to 350°F. Wrap the outside of a 9-inch spring-form pan with aluminum foil to prevent leaking.

Sift together the flour, baking powder, baking soda, cinnamon, and salt. Set aside.

In a saucepan over medium heat, combine the brown sugar and margarine. Bring to a boil, then pour into the bottom of the spring-form pan. Sprinkle with the cranberries and pecans.

In a large bowl, blend the oil and sugar with an electric mixer on medium speed until light and fluffy. Beat in the eggs one at a time, and then stir in the vanilla extract. Beat in the flour mixture alternately with the sour cream. Pour the batter into the prepared pan. Bake for 35 to 40 minutes until golden brown.

Yield: 8 servings

DAVE'S FRESH
GINGER CAKE

When Sheilah can't have chocolate, she craves this "best-ever" recipe adapted from David Lebovitz's *Room for Dessert*. David is a well-known chocolate expert and cookbook author, and he leads chocolate tours to France.

2 1/2 cups flour
1 teaspoon ground cinnamon
1/2 teaspoon ground cloves
1/2 teaspoon freshly ground black pepper
1 cup mild unsulphured molasses
1 cup sugar
1 cup canola oil
2 teaspoons baking soda
4 ounces fresh ginger, peeled, sliced, and finely chopped or
    grated
2 large eggs, at room temperature

Place the oven rack in the center of the oven. Preheat the oven to 350°F. Line a 9x3-inch round cake pan or a 9 1/2-inch springform pan with a circle of parchment paper.

In a medium bowl, sift together the flour, cinnamon, cloves, and black pepper. Set aside.

In a large bowl, mix together the molasses, sugar, and oil. Bring 1 cup of water to a boil over high heat in a 2-quart pot. Stir in the baking soda and then mix the hot water into the molasses mixture. Stir in the ginger, mixing well.

Gradually whisk the dry ingredients into the batter. Add the eggs, and continue mixing until everything is thoroughly combined.

Pour the batter into the prepared cake pan and bake for about 1 hour, until the top of the cake springs back lightly when pressed or a cake tester inserted into the center comes out clean. If the top of the cake browns too quickly before the cake is done, drape a piece of foil over the pan and continue baking.

Cool the cake on a wire rack for at least 30 minutes. Run a knife around the edge of the pan to loosen the cake. Remove the cake from the pan and peel off the parchment paper.

Yield: 10 to 12 servings

JEWISH APPLE CAKE

Sheilah receives the most requests for this recipe. Once a former student called Sheilah from India to get a copy! This version also appears in Sheilah's *Simply Irresistible: Easy, Elegant, Fearless, Fussless Cooking.*

Canola oil spray for greasing
3 cups flour, plus additional for dusting
4 to 6 firm Granny Smith or Macintosh apples, peeled and sliced
2 teaspoons ground cinnamon
2 1/4 cups sugar, divided
1 tablespoon baking powder
1 cup canola oil
4 large eggs
1/3 cup freshly squeezed orange juice
1/2 teaspoon salt
2 1/2 teaspoon vanilla extract

Preheat the oven to 350°F. Grease a 10-inch tube pan with the spray and dust with flour.

In a medium bowl, combine the apples with the cinnamon and 1/4 cup of the sugar. Set aside.

In a large bowl, combine the remaining sugar, the 3 cups flour, the baking powder, oil, eggs, orange juice, salt, and vanilla with an electric mixer at medium speed. Beat just until the batter is smooth. Pour a small amount of the batter into the prepared pan, and place a layer of the apple slices on top. Continue layering in this fashion, ending with a layer of batter.

Bake for 1 1/2 hours, or until a cake tester inserted in the center comes out clean. Cool the cake in its pan for 30 minutes on a wire rack; then turn the cake out onto the rack to cool thoroughly.
Yield: 12 servings

GREEK SPICE CAKE

The combination of nuts, moist cake, and syrup will have your friends begging for this recipe. Ellen, a friend Sheilah met while teaching at Jungle Jim's in Cincinnati, shared this family recipe with her; it also appears in her cookbook *Simply Irresistible: Easy, Elegant, Fearless, Fussless Cooking*.

The cake:
Canola spray for greasing
2 cups flour, plus additional for dusting
1 cup canola oil
1 1/2 cups sugar
3 large eggs
3 teaspoons baking powder
1/2 teaspoon baking soda
1 teaspoon ground cinnamon
1/2 teaspoon ground cloves
1 cup milk with 1 teaspoon vinegar mixed in
1 cup chopped walnuts

The syrup:
2 cups sugar
1 cup water
2 cinnamon sticks
1 teaspoon freshly squeezed lemon juice

Preheat the oven to 350°F. Grease a 13x9-inch baking pan with spray and dust with flour.

With an electric mixer, beat the oil and sugar at medium speed for about 3 minutes, until well mixed. Add the eggs, one at a time, beating well after each addition. Add the baking powder, baking soda, cinnamon, and cloves and mix well. With the mixer on its lowest speed, add the 2 cups flour and milk alternately. Stir in the nuts and pour the batter into the prepared pan. Bake for 35 to 40 minutes or until a cake tester inserted in the center comes out clean. Cool in the pan on a wire rack. Cut into diamond shapes.

To prepare the syrup, combine all of the syrup ingredients in a saucepan and bring to a boil. Boil over medium heat for 5 to 7 minutes, stirring constantly. Pour the hot syrup over the cooled cake. Let the cake sit for several hours so all the syrup is absorbed. Remove the cake from the pan and serve the pieces in cupcake papers if desired. *Yield: 12 servings*

Hint: When you are measuring flour or sugar, never use a liquid measuring cup (one with a spout). You cannot get an accurate measure this way. Use dry measuring cups and be sure not to dip them directly into the flour or sugar. Using another cup or spoon, place the loose flour into the measuring cup. Heap it in and level the top with a knife. Liquids should always be measured in a liquid measuring cup and never in dry measuring cups, as the measure will similarly not be accurate.

HELENE'S
CARROT CAKE

Helene's mother and Sheilah's mother were friends, and coincidentally, they were pregnant at the same time. Helene and Sheilah grew up together and both of them love to cook and bake. They have two different styles in the kitchen, however: Sheilah needs to measure everything and Helene just throws ingredients together like grandmother used to do. This is Helene's family's favorite cake.

The cake:
Canola oil for greasing
2 cups flour, plus additional for dusting
2 cups sugar
4 large eggs
1 1/2 cups canola oil
3 cups grated carrots
2 teaspoons cinnamon
2 teaspoons baking soda
1/2 teaspoon salt

The frosting:
1/2 cup canola margarine or butter, at room temperature and cut
    into pieces
1 (8-ounce) package cream cheese, at room temperature and cut
    into pieces
1 teaspoon vanilla extract
1 pound confectioners' sugar
1 cup chopped pecans or walnuts, plus additional for garnish

Preheat the oven to 350°F. Grease 3 8-inch round cake pans with the spray and dust each with flour.

Beat the sugar, eggs, and oil in a food processor. Add the carrots and the remaining cake ingredients. Pulse until well mixed. Scrape down the sides of the food processor occasionally.

Divide the batter evenly among the 3 prepared pans, and bake for 30 to 40 minutes or until a cake tester inserted in the center comes out clean.

When the cakes are cool, prepare the frosting. Add the butter cream cheese, vanilla, sugar, and nuts to a clean food processor and pulse until mixed. Scrape down the sides of the bowl and pulse again.

Place one cake on a serving platter and frost its top. Place the second cake on top and frost its top. Finally place the third cake on top. Spread frosting evenly across the top of the last cake and around the sides of all three layers. Sprinkle with chopped nuts. Store in the refrigerator.

Yield: 12 servings

Hint: When flouring a cake pan, be careful not to overflour. This will only create more crumbs. To avoid overflouring, turn the cake pan over and tap to remove any excess.

LEMON DRIZZLE with
SUNKEN DARK CHOCOLATE CHUNKS

This cake by Deryl Rennie has been adapted from the recipe in Caroline Jeremy's *Green & Black's Chocolate Recipes: From the Cacao Pod to Muffins, Mousses, and Moles* (Kyle Books, 2004). Rennie developed this cake so that she could enjoy her two favorite flavors at once. The pieces of chocolate sink into the batter so that they embed themselves at the bottom of the loaf while the lemon gives the cake a refreshing edge. Using grated chocolate in this recipe will give the cake a speckled appearance.

The cake:
Canola oil spray for greasing
Flour for dusting
1/2 cup canola margarine or butter, at room temperature
1/2 cup sugar
2 large eggs
1 cup self-rising flour
1 teaspoon baking powder
Zest of 1 large lemon
1 tablespoon milk
3 ounces dark chocolate, minimum 60% cocoa content, chopped

The lemon drizzle:
1/4 cup light brown sugar
Juice of 1 lemon

Preheat the oven to 350°F. Grease a 9x5-inch loaf pan with the spray and dust with flour.

In a medium bowl, cream the margarine and sugar with an electric mixer, beating well for 3 or 4 minutes. Add the eggs, one at a time, beating well after each addition. On the mixer's lowest speed or with a rubber spatula, add the flour, baking powder, and lemon zest and mix just until well blended. Stir in the milk to make a soft dropping consistency. Stir in the chocolate. Spoon the mixture into the prepared pan, smooth the surface, and bake for 40 minutes or until the center of the cake springs back when gently pressed.

Stir the light brown sugar into the lemon juice and pour it over the hot cake in its pan. Make a few holes with a fine skewer if the lemon icing remains on the surface instead of soaking into the cake. Remove the cake from its pan and place on a wire rack, leaving it in its paper (if using) to cool completely.

Yield: 10 servings

Hint: Scrape the sides of the bowl often during mixing to create a more uniform batter.

LEMON SCRATCH CAKE
with CITRUS DRIZZLE

This was a staple in Sheri's house as she was growing up, and she has handed this recipe down to her children. In order to omit the trans fats that are so readily found in boxed cake mixes, Sheri makes her cakes from scratch, which she finds hardly takes more time and yields much tastier results.

The cake:
Canola oil spray for greasing
2 1/2 cups flour, plus additional for dusting
1 1/2 cups sugar
2 1/2 teaspoons baking powder
1/2 teaspoon baking soda
1/4 teaspoon salt
1/2 cup freshly squeezed orange juice
1/4 cup freshly squeezed lemon juice
3/4 cup canola oil
1 teaspoon vanilla
4 eggs

The drizzle:
1 3/4 cups powdered sugar
1/2 cup freshly squeezed lemon juice
1 teaspoon lemon zest

Preheat the oven to 325°F. Grease a 9x13-inch baking dish with the spray and dust with flour.

In a large bowl, combine the flour, sugar, baking powder, baking soda, salt, orange juice, lemon juice, oil, vanilla, and eggs. Beat with an electric mixer until combined. Pour the batter into the prepared dish and bake until dark golden brown, about 40 minutes.

While the cake is baking, combine the powdered sugar, lemon juice, and lemon zest and whisk to blend.

Remove the cake from the oven and poke the top liberally with a fork. Stir the drizzle mixture again and carefully spoon it over the cake. Allow cake to cool.

Yield: 12 servings

MANGO CAKE
with CARDAMOM

Kerry Dunnington, caterer, fabulous cook, and cookbook author, is very creative. She developed this cake, for example, when she had too many ripe mangoes. This version is adapted from a recipe in Dunnington's *This Book Cooks* (Xlibris, 2004). The combination of mango and aromatic cardamom makes for a delicious dessert.

Canola spray for greasing
1 cup peeled and chopped mango (about 2 medium mangoes)
1/2 cup raspberry-cranberry juice
2 large eggs
2/3 cup sugar
1 teaspoon vanilla extract
1/4 cup canola margarine or butter, melted
1/4 cup canola oil
1 cup flour
1/2 teaspoon ground cardamom
Confectioners' sugar, optional

Preheat the oven to 400°F. Lightly cover a 10-inch round baking pan with cooking spray. Distribute the mango evenly over the bottom of the pan and pour the juice over the fruit.

In a large bowl, beat the eggs and gradually add the sugar. Mix until well combined. Add the vanilla, margarine, and oil and beat until well combined. Stir in the flour and cardamom, and mix well.

Spoon the batter over the fruit mixture. (The fruit will show through in some places, but cooking will distribute the batter evenly.) Bake for 20 minutes or until light brown and bubbly. Allow the cake to cool and sprinkle with confectioners' sugar if desired.
Yield: 8 servings

Hint: A ripe mango is orange-yellow and rosy blush in color and will give when pressed lightly. Mangoes take about 3 to 4 days to fully ripen.

TWIN BERRY
SHORTCAKES

For Sheri, this recipe brings back many childhood memories as well as memories of her own children and how they would go out to the raspberry patch to pick their berries (while avoiding the bees) and see who could pick the most without eating them all. When they'd returned from the patch, they'd make this summertime dessert to cool them down.

The biscuits:
2 cups whole grain pastry flour
2 teaspoons baking powder
1/2 teaspoon baking soda
1/2 teaspoon salt
2 tablespoons sugar
4 tablespoons canola oil
1 cup buttermilk, well-shaken

The filling:
3 cups raspberries
1 1/2 cups blackberries
2 tablespoons sugar
1 teaspoon orange zest

The cream:
1 cup heavy cream, well-chilled
1 tablespoon powdered sugar

Move the oven rack to the middle position and heat the oven to 450°F. In a large bowl, whisk together the flour, baking powder, baking soda, salt, and sugar. Blend in the oil until the mixture resembles a coarse meal. Add the buttermilk and stir until a soft, sticky dough forms. Drop dough in 6 mounds about 2 inches apart on an ungreased baking sheet. Bake until golden, 12 to 15 minutes. Transfer the biscuits to a rack and cool to warm, about 10 minutes.

While the biscuits bake, gently mash 1 1/2 cups of the raspberries and 3/4 cups of the blackberries with the sugar in a bowl, then stir in the remaining berries and the orange zest. Set aside.

With an electric mixer, beat the cream and the sugar in a large bowl until soft peaks form. Set aside.

When the biscuits have cooled, carefully cut them in half horizontally and arrange the bottom halves, split side up, on each of 6 plates. Top each with berries, whipped cream, and the other half of biscuit. Serve immediately.

Yield: 6 servings

CHAPTER 11

Desserts—
Cookies

FRIED BANANAS

What started as a mock attempt to make indoor banana boats has become quite a tradition in the Coleman house. Sheri's daughters have taken this dessert recipe and experimented with many different toppings. The family's favorite to date is freshly made caramel sauce and whipped cream.

Canola oil for frying
6 medium bananas, firm to touch

Pour 1 inch of oil into an electric skillet and preheat to 375°F. Peel the bananas and split them lengthwise. With a large spatula, carefully lower the banana halves into the oil, no more than 6 at a time. Cook for 2 to 3 minutes, flip the bananas over, and cook for 2 to 3 minutes more until the banana is light golden brown. Carefully remove the bananas and allow to drain on paper towels. Top with chocolate chips, marshmallows, sweetened condensed milk, chopped nuts, caramel, whipped cream, or any of your favorite toppings.
Yield: 6 servings

Hint: When choosing bananas for this recipe, it is best to pick those that have green tips and that are not overripe. They will hold their shape much better when you remove them from the pan.

ALMOND ORANGE BISCOTTI

This is a version of a traditional recipe from Calabria, a fertile coastal region of Italy. Almonds and oranges are two of the locally produced foods highlighted in this crunchy cookie. This version of the recipe offers alternative ingredients to accommodate people with wheat, dairy, and egg allergies. Biscotti made with the allergy-sensitive ingredients crumble easier and therefore must bake longer the second time around. This recipe is courtesy of Amy Riolo.

7 tablespoons canola oil
3/4 cup raw sugar
1 large egg, optional
1/2 cup freshly squeezed orange juice
2 cups oat or all-purpose flour, sifted
2 teaspoons ground cinnamon
1 teaspoon baking soda
1 1/2 teaspoons baking powder
1/2 teaspoon salt
1 cup blanched almonds, chopped roughly
Zest of 2 oranges

Preheat the oven to 350°F. Line a cookie sheet with parchment paper.
In a medium bowl, cream the canola oil and sugar until well blended. Add the egg and mix well. Add the orange juice and mix until well blended. In another medium mixing bowl, combine all of the remaining ingredients. Slowly incorporate the dry ingredients into the wet ingredients.

Pour the dough out onto the prepared cookie sheet. Form it into a 4x12-inch log. Bake in the center of the oven for 25 minutes, or until the dough is firm. Remove from the oven and let cool for 5 minutes.

With a large, serrated knife, cut the log into 1-inch-thick biscotti. The cookies should be cut with one strong motion of the knife. Do not rock the knife back and forth, or the cookies will crumble. Once the entire log has been cut into slices, remove the lining from the cookie sheet. Place the biscotti cut-side down on the baking sheet.

Reduce the heat to 300°F. Bake for another 25 to 30 minutes or until golden and hard. Remove from the oven and cool. Stored in an airtight container, these cookies will last up to two weeks.
Yield: about 2 dozen

CRANBERRY ALMOND BISCOTTI

Canola oil spray for greasing
2 3/4 cups flour
1 cup sugar
1/4 cup dried cranberries
1/4 cup slivered almonds
2 teaspoons baking powder
1/8 teaspoon salt
2 tablespoons canola oil
1 teaspoon almond extract
1 teaspoon vanilla extract
3 large eggs

Preheat the oven to 350°F. Coat a cookie sheet with canola spray.

In a large bowl, combine the flour, sugar, cranberries, almonds, baking powder, and salt. In a small bowl, combine the oil, almond extract, vanilla extract, and eggs. Add the oil mixture to the flour mixture and stir until well blended. The dough will be dry and crumbly.

Place the dough on a lightly floured surface and knead lightly 8 to 10 times. Divide the dough into half. Shape each portion into an 8-inch-long roll. Place the rolls 4 inches apart on the prepared cookie sheet. Flatten the rolls to a 1-inch thickness. Bake for 35 minutes.

Remove the rolls from the cookie sheet and cool on a rack for 10 minutes. Cut each roll diagonally into 15 slices. Place slices cut-side down on the cookie sheet. Reduce the oven temperature to 325°F and bake for an additional 10 minutes. Remove the biscotti from the cookie sheet and cool completely on a wire rack.
Yield: 30 biscotti

Hint: Eggs should not be washed at home. They are washed and sanitized before being packed. Incorrect washing could contaminate the eggshell's contents. Cracked or leaking eggs should be discarded because cracks allow bacteria to enter through the shell, even if the egg is not leaking.

CRANBERRY
SHORTBREAD BARS

This recipe is Sheri's attempt to replicate her favorite dessert bar from her favorite coffee place. These bars can be made throughout the year, but they are best in the winter months with a nice cup of coffee or tea.

Canola oil spray
1 cup canola margarine
1/2 cup confectioners' sugar
1 egg
1 1/2 cups flour
Dash of salt
1/2 cup sugar
1/2 cup packed brown sugar
3 tablespoons cornstarch
1 (12-ounce) package fresh cranberries
1 teaspoon orange zest
1 cup unsweetened apple juice
1 cup chopped pecans
2 (1-ounce) squares white baking chocolate, melted

Preheat the oven to 425°F. Grease a 13x9-inch baking dish with the spray.

In a large bowl, mix the margarine and confectioners' sugar. Beat in the egg. Combine the flour and salt, and gradually add to the creamed mixture. Set aside 1 cup of these crumbs for the topping. Spread the remaining mixture in the prepared dish. Bake for 10 minutes.

Combine the sugar, brown sugar, and cornstarch in a small saucepan. Stir in the cranberries, orange zest, and apple juice. Bring to a boil over high heat. Reduce the heat and cook, stirring, for 5 minutes or until thickened. Remove the sauce from heat and stir in the pecans.

Spread the sauce over the crust. Sprinkle with the reserved crumb mixture. Bake for 10 to 25 minutes or until golden brown and bubbly. Cool on a wire rack. Drizzle with white chocolate. Cut into bars.
Yield: 3 dozen

ENGLISH COOKIES

The hazelnuts in this recipe bring an extra level to this modified chocolate chip cookie that tingles the taste buds. These cookies are best if you use a good brand of chocolate, such as Scharffen Berger, Vosges, or Lindt.

1/3 cup canola oil
1/4 cup soft brown sugar
1/4 cup superfine sugar
1 egg, lightly beaten
Two drops almond extract
1 1/2 cups flour
2 teaspoons baking powder
Pinch of salt
2 tablespoons milk, or as needed
1/2 cup shelled hazelnuts, coarsely chopped
2 ounces semisweet chocolate, coarsely chopped

Preheat the oven to 350°F.

In a large bowl, cream the oil with the sugars. Beat in the egg and almond extract. Combine the flour, baking powder, and salt in another bowl; then sift the dry ingredients into the sugar mixture, beating constantly with a wooden spoon. If necessary, soften the mixture with a little milk. Stir in the hazelnuts and chocolate.

Drop tablespoonfuls of the dough 1 to 2 inches apart on an ungreased cookie sheet and bake for about 7 to 8 minutes. Remove the cookie sheet from the oven and let the cookies cool slightly. Remove the cookies with a spatula and let them finish cooling on a wire rack.
Yield: 2 dozen

GRANDMA'S CRAZY
CRUNCH

This recipe was a staple at Sheri's grandmother's house every Christmas holiday as Sheri was growing up. She loves the memories that she creates with this very simple treat with her children now.

2 quarts popped corn
1 1/3 cups pecans
2/3 cup slivered almonds
1 1/3 cups sugar
1 cup canola margarine
1 teaspoon vanilla
1/2 cup corn syrup

Combine the popped corn, pecans, and almonds in a large mixing bowl. Combine the remaining ingredients in a saucepan over medium-high heat and bring to a boil. Boil for 10 minutes and remove from heat. Add the vanilla. Pour the syrup over the corn and nut mixture. Dry on a cookie sheet for several hours, break apart into bite-size pieces, and store in airtight container.

Yield: 10 to 12 servings

ICE CREAM
TREASURE BARS

This is a favorite dessert of the Coleman children, who were excellent testers for many of the recipes in this book. Any flavor of ice cream can be substituted for the vanilla.

5 cups coarsely crushed corn flakes
3/4 cup grated coconut
3/4 cup brown sugar
1/2 cup canola margarine, melted
4 cups vanilla ice cream, plus additional as needed

In a large bowl combine the corn flakes, coconut, and brown sugar. Stir in the melted margarine and mix well to combine.

Remove the ice cream from the freezer and let it melt a bit so you can easily spread it.

Place half of the corn flake mixture in an 11x9-inch pan or baking dish and press gently to form a crust. Using an ice cream scoop or large spoon, begin spreading the ice cream over the crust. Gently smooth the ice cream. Top with the remaining corn flake mixture and cover. Place the bars in the freezer and freeze for several hours. Remove and let sit for a few minutes before serving.

Yield: 16 bars

MOLASSES COOKIES

These cookies are easy and elegant and they freeze beautifully.

1 1/2 cups canola oil
3 cups sugar, divided
2 large eggs
1/2 cup molasses
1 teaspoon ground cloves
1 teaspoon ground ginger
1 teaspoon kosher salt
2 teaspoons ground cinnamon
1 1/2 tablespoons baking soda
3 cups flour, plus additional as needed
Sugar for coating

In a large mixing bowl, beat the oil, 2 cups of the sugar, the eggs, and the molasses with an electric mixer until light in color, about 3 to 5 minutes. In another bowl, combine the cloves, ginger, salt, cinnamon, and baking soda. Add the spice mixture to the dough and mix well. Add the flour slowly, mixing on the lowest speed. Place the dough in a bowl, cover, and refrigerate for 2 to 3 hours, or overnight.

Preheat the oven to 375°F. Place the remaining sugar in a pie pan. Roll the dough in between your palms into 1-inch balls. If the dough is too loose to roll, add a bit more flour. Dip the balls in the sugar, and place them on an ungreased cookie sheet. Bake for 8 to 10 minutes. *Yield: about 4 dozen cookies.*

ROGGIE WEINRAUB'S MANDEL BREAD

This recipe, by Sheilah's mother, creates a much-loved cookie that is similar to biscotti. Whenever Ms. Weinraub is invited somewhere, she's asked to bring her mandel bread. This recipe also appears in Sheilah's *Sephardic Israeli Cuisine: A Mediterranean Mosaic* (Hippocrene Books, 2002).

Canola oil spray for greasing
3 large eggs
3/4 cup sugar
3/4 cup canola oil
2 teaspoons vanilla extract
3 1/2 cups flour
3 teaspoons baking powder
1/2 teaspoon salt
I cup chopped walnuts
Cinnamon-sugar for dusting

Preheat the oven to 350°F. Grease a cookie sheet with the spray.

Using a mixer, beat the eggs and slowly add the sugar to them, mixing well. Add the oil and vanilla and continue beating. Sift together the flour, baking powder, and salt. Sift 3 times. Slowly add the flour mixture to the batter, and beat just to combine. Add the nuts.

Divide the dough in half and shape each half into a log. Place on the prepared cookie sheet. Bake for 20 minutes.

Remove the logs from the oven and slice them while hot. Sprinkle the cookies with cinnamon-sugar. Reduce the oven temperature to 325°F and bake for another 10 minutes, until the cookies are brown and dry.

Yield: 24 cookies

SUGAR COOKIES

To save time, these cookies do not have to be rolled out. This is courtesy of a friend who does not remember where she got it.

1 cup canola margarine
1 cup canola oil
1 cup granulated sugar
1 cup confectioners' sugar
2 large eggs, lightly beaten
2 teaspoons vanilla extract
1 teaspoon lemon extract
4 1/2 cups sifted flour
1 teaspoon baking soda
1 teaspoon cream of tartar
1/2 teaspoon salt

Preheat the oven to 350°F.

Using an electric mixer on medium speed, cream the margarine, oil, sugars, eggs, and vanilla and lemon extracts until smooth and well blended, about 3 to 5 minutes. With mixer on the lowest speed, add the remaining ingredients, beating just until blended.

Using your hands, pinch off pieces of dough, about 2 1/2 to 3 tablespoons each, and roll into balls. Place the balls on an ungreased cookie sheet about 1 1/2 inches apart. Using a fork, gently press the balls down a little. Bake for 10 to 12 minutes. Do not let the cookies brown.

Yield: about 3 dozen cookies

SUGAR COOKIES
with DRIED CHERRIES

Nothing beats a cookie with cherries and white chocolate. This recipe brings raves at the Coleman house.

4 cups flour
1 teaspoon baking powder
1/2 teaspoon salt
3/4 cup canola oil
2 cups sugar
2 large eggs
2 teaspoons almond extract
1 cup finely chopped dried cherries
1 cup white chocolate chips
1 cup coarsely chopped pecans
3 egg whites, gently fork whipped
Sanding sugar

Preheat the oven to 325°F. Line a baking sheet with parchment paper.

Sift the flour, baking powder, and salt into a medium bowl.

In a large bowl, blend the oil and sugar with an electric mixer on medium speed until well combined. Add the eggs and mix well. Stir in almond extract. Add the flour mixture in 3 batches, mixing on low speed after each addition. Add the cherries, white chocolate, and pecans and beat on low until incorporated, 1 to 2 minutes.

Divide the dough in half and roll each half into a 1 1/2- to 2-inch diameter log. Wrap in plastic. Place in the freezer until firm.

Cut the logs into 1/4-inch-thick rounds and place the rounds on the prepared baking sheet. Brush the tops with the egg whites and sprinkle with sanding sugar. Bake until the edges begin to turn golden, 15 to 20 minutes.

Yield: 3 dozen

VERA'S CARAMEL
CANOLA BROWNIES

This recipe was brought to the United States by Vera DahlQuist in 1908, when she emigrated from Finland as a youngster. DahlQuist was a gifted baker, and her caramel canola brownie has a nice chewiness that almost resembles that of soft toffee. To order canola seeds, contact the Northern Canola Growers Association (www.northerncanola.com).

Canola oil spray for greasing
2 1/2 cups flour
3 cups brown sugar
3 teaspoons baking powder
1/4 teaspoon salt
4 eggs
1 1/4 cups canola oil
1 teaspoon vanilla extract
1 cup chopped walnuts or pecans, toasted
1/4 cup canola seeds, toasted

Preheat the oven to 350°F. Grease a 13x9-inch baking pan with the spray and cover with a layer of parchment paper.

In a large mixing bowl, combine the flour, brown sugar, baking powder, and salt. In a small bowl, beat the eggs lightly. Stir the oil and vanilla into the eggs. Add the egg mixture to the dry ingredients and blend well. Stir in the nuts and seeds.

Spread the batter into the prepared pan. Bake for 25 to 30 minutes, or until the center springs back when lightly touched. Be careful not to overbake. Let cool on a wire race and slice.

Yield: 12 to 16 servings

CHAPTER 12

Desserts— Pies

PIECRUST
(with CANOLA OIL)

Traditional piecrust is made with shortening, which is high in saturated and trans fat. Substituting canola oil for shortening replaces those bad fats with little saturated fat and a lot of healthy monounsaturated fat. This crust is so flaky and tasty—with none of the guilt—that you will love it.

3/4 cup whole grain pastry flour
3/4 cup all-purpose flour
1/2 teaspoon salt
1/2 cup canola oil
2 tablespoons white vinegar

Sift together the flours and salt. Form a well in the flour mixture. Add the oil and vinegar and combine until crumbly. Form the dough into a ball. Place the ball of dough on two sheets of nonstick plastic wrap. Cover the ball with another two sheets of nonstick plastic wrap. With a rolling pin, roll the dough to 1/4 inch or desired thickness. Place the unbaked crust into a pie plate and crimp the edges. Prebake at 350°F for 8 minutes or add filling and bake according to pie recipe.
Yield: 1 9-inch deep dish piecrust

Hint: This crust is delicate and not recommended for lattice tops. Use care when placing in pie plate and crimping edge.

APPLE WALNUT PIE

This pie is a decadent old Kaufman family favorite. It also appears in Sheilah Kaufman's *Simply Irresistible: Easy, Elegant, Fearless, Fussless Cooking.*

The filling:
6 or 7 Rome or Beauty apples, peeled, cored, and sliced by hand
1 1/4 cups sour cream
1/2 cup flour
1 large egg
3/4 cup sugar
1 teaspoon vanilla extract
1 recipe Piecrust (made with canola oil), unbaked (see page 213)

The topping:
1/4 cup brown sugar
1/4 cup granulated sugar
1/2 cup flour
6 tablespoons canola margarine
2 cups chopped walnuts

Preheat the oven to 350°F.

To prepare the filling, combine the apples, sour cream, flour, egg, sugar, and vanilla in a large bowl. Let mixture sit for 10 minutes and pour into the 10-inch piecrust.

Combine the topping ingredients and pack over the filling.

Cover the pie with foil and bake the pie for 30 minutes. Remove the foil and continue baking for an additional 30 to 45 minutes, or until the topping is lightly browned.

When the pie is done, remove it from the oven and cool on a wire rack. Then transfer it to the refrigerator. Do not serve or cut for 24 hours. Serve at room temperature.

Yield: 8 to 10 servings

CHOCOLATE RUM
PECAN PIE

1/3 cup cocoa powder
2 tablespoons canola oil
2 ounces canola margarine, melted
4 large eggs, lightly beaten
1 cup sugar
1 1/4 cups dark corn syrup
1 teaspoon vanilla extract
4 tablespoons dark rum
8 ounces chopped pecans
1 recipe Piecrust (made with canola oil), prebaked and cooled
    (see page 213)

Preheat the oven to 350°F.

In a small bowl combine the cocoa, oil, and melted margarine. Set aside.

In a large bowl, beat the eggs with an electric mixer at medium speed. Slowly add the sugar and corn syrup, beating well. Add the cocoa mixture, and stir in the vanilla, rum, and nuts. Blend well and pour into the cooled piecrust. Bake for 50 minutes.

Remove from the oven and cool on a wire rack. Serve slightly chilled or at room temperature.

Yield: 8 servings

CUSTARD TART
with FRESH BERRIES

This recipe combines Sheri's favorite three ingredients: cookie crust, custard, and fresh summer berries. This tart is best in summer when berries are at their peak.

The crust:
1 1/4 cups flour
3 tablespoons sugar
1/4 teaspoon salt
1/3 cup canola oil
1 large egg yolk
1 tablespoon whipping cream

The filling:
1/2 cup whipping cream
2 tablespoons cornstarch
2 large eggs
4 large egg yolks
1 teaspoon vanilla extract
1/2 cup white balsamic vinegar
3/4 cup sugar
1/4 cup canola margarine

The topping:
2 large strawberries, sliced
1 pint blueberries
1/2 pint raspberries

To make the crust, combine the flour, sugar, and salt in a food processor and blend for 5 seconds. Add the oil and pulse on and off until a coarse meal forms. Add the egg yolk and cream and pulse until moist clumps form. Gather the dough into ball. Press the dough evenly into a 9-inch tart pan with a removable bottom. Pierce the dough all over with a fork. Chill for 1 hour.

Preheat the oven to 375°F. Bake the crust until golden, about 20 minutes, pressing with back of fork if it begins to bubble. Cool.

To make the filling, combine the cream and cornstarch in medium bowl until the cornstarch dissolves. Add the egg yolks and vanilla and whisk to blend. Bring the vinegar to a boil in a heavy medium saucepan. Boil until reduced to 1/4 cup, about 3 minutes. Add 3/4 cup water, sugar, and margarine to the vinegar. Stir until the margarine melts and return the mixture to a boil. Gradually whisk the vinegar mixture into the egg mixture and return to the saucepan. Whisk until the custard thickens and boils. Strain into a bowl. Cool. Spread the custard in the prepared crust. Cover and chill the tart at least 3 hours.

Mix fruit together and place on top of the custard.

Yield: 6 to 8 servings

GLADY'S MAGIC BLUEBERRY PIE

This recipe is a Coleman family favorite that just can't be beat, especially in the summer season when blueberries are at their peak. Sheri can still remember going blueberry picking with her mother and grandmother in Wisconsin in 1970, each of them with a bucket in hand.

1 (15-ounce) can sweetened condensed milk
1/4 cup freshly squeezed lemon juice
2 egg yolks
2 cups fresh blueberries
3 egg whites
2 tablespoons sugar
1 teaspoon cream of tartar
1 recipe Piecrust (made with canola oil), prebaked (see page 213)

Preheat the oven to 400°F.

Blend the condensed milk, lemon juice, and egg yolks together until thickened. Gently fold in the blueberries. Pour into the piecrust.
Place the egg whites, sugar, and cream of tartar in a bowl and beat with an electric mixer until stiff peaks form. Spread the meringue over the blueberry filling.

Bake the pie for 10 minutes or until the meringue peaks are golden brown.

Yield: 6 to 8 servings

MAI TAI PIE

If you have a passion for flavor, this low-fat pie is for you. The combination of pineapple, rum, and lime will let you believe you are on a Caribbean island. Sheilah learned this terrific recipe from cooking teacher Jill Sullivan who taught low-fat cooking classes before she moved to Hawaii.

1 (20-ounce) can crushed pineapple, with juice
1/4 cup cornstarch
Pinch of salt
1/4 cup dark rum
1 cup sugar
4 eggs or 1 cup egg substitute
Zest and freshly squeezed juice of 1 lime
5 large egg whites
1 recipe Piecrust (made with canola oil), unbaked (see page 213)

Preheat the oven to 350°F.

In a medium saucepan, combine the pineapple, cornstarch, salt, rum, and 3/4 cup of the sugar. Cook over medium heat, stirring, until the mixture starts to boil. Remove the pan from the heat. Stir a couple of tablespoons of the hot pineapple mixture into the eggs. Pour the egg mixture back into the pineapple mixture and stir to combine. Return the mixture to heat and cook 1 to 2 minutes more, stirring constantly, until it just begins to simmer. Stir in the lime zest and juice. Remove from heat and cool to room temperature.

Place the egg whites in a large bowl and beat with an electric mixer until they hold soft peaks. Sprinkle the remaining sugar over the top of the egg whites and continue to beat until they form stiff peaks. Fold 1 cup of the beaten egg whites into the pineapple mixture. Pour the filling into the piecrust and bake until set, approximately 15 minutes. Spread the remaining stiff egg whites over the top of the baked pie and bake for 10 minutes more, or until the meringue is lightly browned. Serve immediately.

Yield: 8 servings

Hint: In a standard large egg, the white is 2 tablespoons and the yolk is one tablespoon. Most recipes are based on large eggs.

VERY BERRY PIE

This recipe is simple and quick, but it's eaten just as quickly.

1 recipe Piecrust (made with canola oil), fully baked and cooled
       (see page 213)
1 quart strawberries, blueberries, blackberries, raspberries, or a
       mixture of any of these
 2 tablespoons cornstarch
3/4 cup sugar
1 (3-ounce) box fruit gelatin to match the berries used

Place the berries in the cooled, baked piecrust. In a pot over medium heat, combine 1 1/2 cups water, cornstarch, and sugar. Cook, stirring, until the liquid is clear and the sugar is dissolved. Stir in the gelatin and continue cooking another minute or two, until the gelatin is dissolved. Pour the glaze over the fruit and let cool. Cover and refrigerate overnight.

Serve with whipped topping if desired.

Yield: 6 servings

PUMPPLE
CRUMBLE PIE

This pumpkin and apple pie was a winner at the Remsen Festival in upstate New York several years ago.

1 recipe Piecrust (made with canola oil), unbaked (see page 213)

The pumpkin filling:
2 eggs, slightly beaten
1 1/2 cups pureed pumpkin
I cup evaporated milk
1/2 cup sugar
2 tablespoons canola margarine, melted
3/4 teaspoon cinnamon
1/8 teaspoon nutmeg
1/4 teaspoon salt

The apple filling:
2 medium apples, peeled, cored, and sliced
1/4 cup sugar
1 teaspoon flour
I teaspoon freshly squeezed lemon juice
1/4 teaspoon cinnamon

The topping:
1/2 cup flour
5 tablespoons brown sugar
3 tablespoons softened canola margarine
1/3 cup chopped walnuts

Preheat the oven to 375°F. Place the piecrust in a 9- or 10-inch pie pan. Flute the edges with a fork.

In a medium bowl, combine all of the ingredients for the pumpkin filling and set aside.

In another bowl, combine the apples with the sugar, flour, lemon juice, and cinnamon. Place the apple filling in the bottom of the prepared piecrust. Pour the pumpkin mixture over the apples and bake for 30 minutes.

Combine the topping ingredients until crumbly and sprinkle over the pie. Continue baking for 20 more minutes.

Let the pie cool on a wire rack until lukewarm.

Yield: 6 to 8 servings

WHITE CHOCOLATE BERRY PIE

Any fresh berries will work in this delicious pie.

1 recipe Piecrust (made with canola oil), prebaked and cooled
    (see page 213)
5 (1-ounce) squares white chocolate, divided
2 tablespoons milk
4 ounces cream cheese, softened
1/3 cup sifted confectioners' sugar
1 teaspoon orange zest
1 cup heavy cream
2 cups fresh raspberries or sliced strawberries

In a microwave-safe bowl, place 4 squares of the chocolate and the milk. Microwave for one minute on high. Remove the chocolate from the microwave and stir. If the chocolate is not fully melted, return it to the microwave for another 15 seconds. Remove and stir again. Repeat until the chocolate is melted. Set it aside to cool to room temperature.

In a medium bowl, beat the cream cheese, confectioners' sugar, and orange zest with an electric mixer on low speed until smooth. Beat in the cooled white chocolate mixture.

In another bowl, whip the cream with an electric mixer on high speed until stiff peaks form. Gently fold the whipped cream into the chocolate mixture. Spoon the filling into the piecrust, and arrange the berries on top.

Melt the remaining square of chocolate in the microwave as before and drizzle on top. Refrigerate for at least 1 hour before serving.

Yield: 6 servings

INDEX

A

Almond Orange Biscotti, 202
Apple Walnut Pie, 214
Applesauce Loaf, 157
Artichoke Hearts with Chilies, Garlic, and Balsamic Vinegar, 1
Asian-Style Honey Vegetable Stir-Fry, 129

B

Baby Greens with Maple Citrus Dressing, 110
Bacon and Mushrooms with Spinach over Creamy Polenta, 60
Baked Chicken Parmesan, 41
Baked Fennel Parmesan, 130
Baked Grouper Fillet with Roasted Tomatoes, 98
Baked Tomatoes Stuffed with Couscous, 132
Balsamic Canola Glaze, 61
Barbecued Veal Chops with Macadamia Nuts, 62
Bean Purses, 2
Beef with Oyster Sauce, 64
Bell Pepper Stir-Fry, 80
Best Baked Potatoes, 134
Black Bean Chili, 79
Black Olive Tapenade, 3
Blackened Tuna, 99
Bread Cup Eggs, 81
Broccoli and Cheese Fritters, 131

Brussels Sprouts with Pancetta, 135
Buttermilk Prune Cake, 179

C

Cajun Fries, 136
Caramel Sauce, 177
Caramelized Onion Focaccia, 158
Caramelized Potato Kugel, 137
Cashew Chicken with Broccoli and Red Bell Peppers, 38
Celery and Mushroom Bake, 138
Cherry Breakfast Bake, 180
Chicken Breasts Caribbean,
Chicken Breasts Romano, 44
Chicken Cacciatore, 46
Chicken Dijon, 47
Chicken Fiesta Casserole, 48
Chili Con Carne, 25
Chili Corn Chowder, 26
Chili Pecans, 3
Chinese Steak with Pea Pods, 63
Chinese Noodles with Chicken, 49
Chinese Oven Rice, 139
Chocolate Carrot Cake, 182
Chocolate Chip Banana Bread, 159
Chocolate Mousse Cake, 184
Chocolate Port Sauce, 178
Chocolate Pudding Cake, 181
Chocolate Rum Pecan Pie, 215
Classic Three-Bean Salad, 111
Clifton Beach Salad Dressing, 109
Cold Marinated Vegetables, 112

Crab Wontons, 4
Cranberry Almond Biscotti, 203
Cranberry Pudding Cake, 186
Cranberry Shortbread Bars, 204
Cranberry Upside Down Cake, 187
Cranberry Vinaigrette, 110
Creamed Whipped Potatoes, 140
Curried Sweet Potatoes, 141
Custard Tart with Fresh Berries, 216

D
Dave's Fresh Ginger Cake, 188
Dried Breadcrumbs, 95

E
Egg Souffle, 82
Eggplant and Chickpea Tagine, 84
Eggplant Spread, 5
English Cookies, 205

F
Fennel Plain and Simple, 133
Ferne's Healthy Borscht, 27
Fig and Ginger Chicken Breasts with
    Couscous, 50
Fish Tacos, 100
Flank Steak with Wild Mushrooms and
    Herbs, 59
Fresh Asparagus with Wild Mushrooms
    and Roasted Peppers, 142
Fresh Tomato Salsa, 6
Fresh Tomato Tart, 83
Fried Bananas, 201
Fried Goat Cheese with Mint, 7

G
Gazpacho, 28
Glady's Magic Blueberry Pie, 217
Gorgonzola Lemon Rice, 143
Grandma's Crazy Crunch, 206
Grape and Cranberry Tea Bread, 160
Greek Spice Cake, 190
Greek-Style Marinated Mushrooms, 8
Green Olive and Walnut Spread, 9
Grilled Chicken with Honey Mustard, 37
Grilled Halibut, 102

Grilled Pineapple and Goat Cheese, 10
Grilled Stuffed Portobello Mushrooms, 85
Grilled Tomatoes with Goat Cheese, 11
Grilled Tuna Schwarma Kebabs, 101
Ground Beef with Eggplant in Garlic
    Sauce, 65
Grown-Up Macaroni and Cheese, 86

H
Helene's Carrot Cake, 192
Herbed Corn Muffins, 161
Herbed Garlic Bread, 171
Herbed Green Beans, 144
Herbed Mushrooms with Wine Sauce,
    145
Herbed Pan-Fried Fish, 104
Herbed Spread, 175
Honey Chicken Wings, 14
Honey Doughnuts, 162
Honeydew Walnut Salad, 113

I
Ice Cream Treasure Bars, 207

J
Jalapeño Chicken Soup with Shiitake
    Matzo Balls, 30
Jewish Apple Cake, 189
Jicama and Papaya Salad, 114
Jonathan Krinn's 2941 Mushroom
    Soup, 29

K
Kerry's Delicious Biscuits, 163

L
Lamb Racks with Herbed Pine Nut
    Crust, 66
Lamb with Prunes, 67
Layered Southwest Chicken Salad, 52
Leek and Apple Tarts, 12
Lemon Drizzle with Sunken Dark
    Chocolate Chunks, 194
Lemon Herb Grilled Steak, 69
Lemon Scratch Cake with Citrus
    Drizzle, 196

Lentil and Spinach Salad, 115

M

Macaroni with Chicken, 54
Mai Tai Pie, 218
Mango Cake with Cardamom, 197
Mango Chicken Quesadillas, 51
Marcia Macomb's Stir-Fried Asparagus, 134
Marinated Flank Steak, 73
Marinated Mushrooms Greek-style, 8
Marinated Olives, 14
Mexican Chicken Soup, 33
Michelle's Famous Chicken Pot Pie, 56
Mimosa Cauliflower Salad, 116
Molasses Cookies, 208
Mom's Crock-Pot Stuffing, 146
Moussaka, 88
Mushroom and Spinach Casserole, 90
Mushroom Mock Chopped Liver, 13

N

North Dakota German Potato Salad, 119

O

Oranges in Honey, 117
Oriental Chicken Stir-Fry, 39
Oven-Seared Marinated Salmon, 97

P

Pakistani-Style Lamb Patties, 68
Pan-Fried Zucchini with Tahini Dressing, 148
Parmesan Skillet Cornbread, 164
Pear, Gorgonzola, and Toasted Walnut Strudel, 15
Pesto Cheese Party Mold, 16
Picadillo, 70
Picnic Bean Salad, 118
Piecrust, 213
Poppy Seed Bread, 165
Pork and Prunes a la Loire, 72
Port Sauce, 61
Potato and Cauliflower Mash, 149
Pumpkin Ribbon Bread, 166
Pumpple Crumble Pie, 220

R

Raspberry Spread, 175
Ratatouille Casserole, 150
Red Bell Pepper and Fennel Soup, 32
Red, White, and Blue Potato Salad, 120
Rice Tabbouleh, 139
Rio Bravo Rice-Stuffed Poblanos, 151
Roasted Garlic Spread, 17
Roasted Pumpkin and Spinach Penne, 87
Roasted Red Bell Pepper Hummus, 18
Roasted Squash Soup, 34
Roggie Weinraub's Mandel Bread, 209
Rustic Pasta with Tomatoes, Olives, and Ricotta, 91

S

Salmon and Blueberry Salad with Red Onion Vinaigrette, 103
Salmon Bake with Pecan-Crunch Topping, 105
Salmon Fillet with Squash and Kumquats, 106
Sanganaki, 19
Satay, 74
Sheri's Favorite Pumpkin Bread, 174
Sheri's Hungarian Stew, 35
Shrimp Creole, 108
Smoked Gouda and Spinach Rice Casserole, 152
Soft Granola, 167
Southwestern-Style Quiche, 75
Spice-It-Up Orange Chicken, 53
Spiced Maple Spread, 175
Spiced Salad Croutons, 121
Spicy Grilled Chicken, 43
Spicy Three-Pepper Hummus, 20
Spinach Dill Latkes, 153
Spinach, Rice, and Feta Pie, 92
Spinach Salad with Citrus Vinaigrette, 122
Spinach Salad with Grapes and Oranges, 123
Split Pea Soup with Ham Hock, 36
Stone-Ground Whole Wheat Bread, 168

Stuffed Cabbage, 71
Stuffed Mini Bell Peppers, 21
Sugar Cookies, 210
Sugar Cookies with Dried Cherries,
    211
Sweet and Sour Carrots, 154
Sweet Onion Rolls, 170
Sweet Potato Bake, 155
Sweet Potato Frites, 145

T
Tex-Mex Latkes, 22
Tofu Chili, 93
Tom Douglas's Fabulous Potato Latkes
    with Lemon Dill Cream, 94
Tomato and Basil Pasta Salad, 124
Tostadas Mexicano, 76
Trout with Almonds, 107
Twin Berry Shortcakes, 198

U
Uncle Menashe's Magic Challah, 172

V
Vera's Caramel Canola Brownies, 212
Very Berry Pie, 219

W
Watermelon and Red Onion Salad, 126
White Chocolate Berry Pie, 221
Wild Rice Salad, 125

Y
Yankee Pot Roast, 77

Z
Zesty Bread Dipper, 17
Zucchini Bites, 23
Zucchini Bread, 169

ABOUT THE AUTHORS

Sheilah Kaufman is a nationally recognized author of twenty-five cookbooks, including the acclaimed *Simply Irresistible: Easy, Elegant, Fearless, Fussless Cooking*; *A Taste of Turkish Cuisine*; *Sephardic Israeli Cuisine*; and *Soups, Stews, and Chowders*, as well as her most recent *Upper Crusts: Fabulous Ways to Use Bread*. She is renowned for her user-friendly style and her easy, elegant, and innovative recipes. Sheilah has been a culinary instructor for more than thirty-eight years and continues to teach gourmet-cooking classes across the country. She is the Web food editor for Jewish Women International, a contributing food writer for the *Washington Post* and *Vegetarian Times Magazine*, and the food editor for the *Town Courier*, as well as a freelance writer and editor. She has developed recipes for Beatrice Foods, Smucker's, and Gourmet Delight and created the "Cheater's Diet" for Walden Farms. She was the Food and Gift Basket Editor for *Gift & Decorative Accessories* magazine for more than twenty years. In other words, Sheilah knows her way around the kitchen and, more important, how to share her secrets with an every-day audience. She is a founding member of the International Association of Culinary Professionals and a member of Les Dames d'Escoffier, Slow Foods, Chow, and a number of writers' organizations. Sheilah Kaufman lives in Potomac, Maryland. www.cookingwithsheilah.com.

Sheri L. Coleman, BSN, RN, epitomizes the proverbial "from farm to market" phrase. She grew up on a farm and livestock operation in southwestern North Dakota and is currently the director of marketing and health promotion for the Northern Canola Growers Association. In this capacity she is responsible for educating consumers, both domestic and international, on the health benefits of canola oil. En route to her current position, Sheri became a registered nurse and acquired extensive experience in healthcare. By working in public health and direct patient care, she has practiced preventative medicine, has been involved in education, and has been responsible for program management. Sheri also writes a health column, "Ask Sheri," for several journals and newspapers. Sheri, who currently lives in Bismarck, North Dakota, with her husband and their four children, fully appreciates what life has to offer and is enjoying the culinary adventures that go along with it.